C000216616

Nightwalk

Nightwalk
Chris Yates
A Journey to the
Heart of Nature

Collins

CONTENTS

TO MY BROTHER NICK, WHO,
IN OUR BOYHOOD, OFTEN WALKED
THE NIGHT PATH WITH ME.

'To walk for hours
on a clear night is the
largest experience we
can have'

IN PRAISE OF WALKING,
BY THOMAS A. CLARK

1

WHEN TIME
SLOWS DOWN

Time is short in midwinter, ticking along at the same pace as a man hurrying towards a railway station, but in midsummer time is long and if the man could adjust his pace accordingly he would always miss his train.

From mid June to mid July I hardly ever think about catching trains or buses or anything else that runs to the tick of the clock, but I do think about catching fish because the season on my favourite waters begins at this time and therefore, being a devout angler, I cannot help slowing to the pulse of midsummer as I re-enter a world of quiet ponds, reflected evenings and misted dawns. Since I fledged and learnt to cast a line, half a century ago, I have never failed to return, like a migratory bird, to my summer angling, yet even I appreciate that when the days extend there is time to do more than just fish. Despite my seasonal obsession, I know an evening will come, sometime around the solstice, when all thoughts of fish simply swim away and I shall be drawn instead towards another equally compelling idea.

As I write this my rods and tackle are strewn untidily around the room. I am sitting by a window, keeping half an eye on the twin oak trees that stand high up on a slope opposite my house. At the moment their foliage is smouldering gold in the light of the setting sun; soon it will revert to a uniform green before fading through all the blues to grey. Finally, in about an hour, both trees will stand black and formless against the twilight, like cartoon impressions of themselves, and only then, when the whole landscape is in silhouette, will I set out – not to fish, but to walk across the narrow midsummer night until the sun reappears in the morning.

Unlike my stillwater angling, which always begins on the sixteenth of June, the nocturnal stroll is a more random event, though its timing does not depend on how good or bad the fishing has been. As I said, it usually happens near the solstice, when the night at this latitude is just a four-hour band of shadow, but if the conditions are unsuitable I will wait until the weather is benign, the air calm and the moon reasonable. For over a month now the airstream has been northerly and the skies clear. The days have been hot, but without atmosphere; the nights have been cold and when the moon was last full it cast a brittle, almost wintry, light. It might seem churlish to be sniffy about cool, clear nights when summer weather is often overcast and soggy, but cold, dry conditions can make the after-dark landscape seem as hollow as an empty shell while mild, soft conditions bring it rustling to life.

Today at about teatime, just as I was thinking of heading back to a lovely willow-cloistered pool, I noticed the distant view from my window suddenly seemed *more* distant. Opening the window wider, I looked up at a single vaguely fish-shaped cloud that was drifting from the south. The air had more density than before; it smelt of grass and elderblossom and the birdsong it carried had more resonance. Any experienced angler will tell you that a mellowing change of weather like this invariably has a sparkling effect on the fish.

This evening, the ponds and lakes will be jumping, but I will be elsewhere.

2

LAST LIGHT

The two trees seem to stand more dominantly on the hill now that the sun has just set. A gang of young rooks almost landed in them a moment ago, spinning round the topmost branches and shouting frantically. Perhaps they had spotted a waking owl or maybe they were thinking of starting a new republic, but after a few overhead sweeps they realized it was getting late and beaked off home to their rookery. It is not really late, though. The clock may be saying almost nine thirty, but with the light sinking so slowly there will be plenty of time to savour this pot of tea and still begin my walk before dark.

I prefer to set off on a night stroll at dusk. Not only can the eyes adjust more effectively than if I stepped directly into full darkness from a lit room, I like the way my familiar surroundings are differently transformed by the twilight as I walk through them. Some things melt into their background, others remain solidly fixed yet reveal surprising new identities. Also, there is sometimes an interesting meeting between diurnal and nocturnal nature, like when early bats and late swallows swoop together or a hare is startled by a badger.

Through my open window the sounds of the evening chorus are diminishing and fragmenting, though the song thrush is chivvying what remains of the choir to 'Keep up! Keep up! Keep up!' I can see him sitting in the top of the yew tree in the corner of my garden, chest puffed out, head back, oblivious now to the other songsters, consumed only with his need to proclaim himself. Since he struck up his first tune at five o'clock this morning he has hardly given himself time to breathe, let alone feed or attend to any domestic chores. No other songbird can match his endurance. Somewhere nearby his mate is sitting on the nest with her second brood. Is she impressed by his epic daily performance? Is she not a little sick of all the endless repetitions of signature phrases? Surely the message has got through by now. Would she not prefer him to offer more help with the children? Occasionally he smashes a snail and brings it to them, but they are not as important as his song.

He is defiant, like a bugle, while a blackbird is seductive, like a flute, and there is one – a real maestro – calling from the apple tree in the other corner of the garden. If the thrush wakes me before sunrise, as he has often done since April, I can sometimes get irritated (I am never in bed till well after midnight), but if this particular blackbird rouses me so early I just smile into my pillow. His tone is unmistakably blackbird, but the improvisations, the liquid looping phrases and the unexpected key changes are his alone. He makes a thrush sound mechanical and a nightingale seem monotonous. (There are no nightingales round here any more, but even if there were, late June is always too late for their song.)

Though the owls – tawny owls – often call in the half-light, they usually allow a short interval after the last songbird before they announce themselves. Depending on their mood and the conditions, they are sometimes mute all night, particularly at this time of year when they have owlets to feed. On other nights, during other seasons, every wood and valley for miles around will be softly echoing to their melancholy voices.

I came to this area with my young family twenty-five years ago, attracted by the rolling chalk downland as much as the streams and rivers that flowed through it. My childhood home was on the North Downs, a hundred miles east, so the topography here seemed familiar despite the hills being higher and the woods more extensive than the ones I used to amble amongst. It is my favourite kind of walking country, and this house, an eighteenth-century estate-worker's cottage, is set right in the heart of it. I can step straight out of my door, climb the tree-hung slope behind the house, and set off along paths and tracks that continue uninterrupted for miles. The only people I am likely to meet in the daytime are occasional fellow walkers, shepherds (on quad bikes) and gamekeepers (in Land Rovers). At night, because I go quietly and never carry a torch, I only ever meet the true natives.

Though this evening's excursion will probably be the only one of the year that leads through to dawn, I have always been enthusiastic about night rambling, even if it is just a short stargazing stroll after supper. My children, too, by accompanying me on moonlit jaunts when they were very young, soon overcame their instinctive fear of the dark and would go on nocturnal adventures of their own.

When I was a child, my parents would take my sister, brother and me for long Sunday walks through the fields and woods that began at the end of our street, but we were nearly always home before dark. In midwinter, however, when the sun sets at four in the afternoon, we would sometimes find that the dark had overtaken us. Though my parents tried to avoid such lateness, I liked the way the orderly landscape seemed to grow wilder and more mysterious as the twilight faded; and I liked how the prospect of darkness chased everyone else away long before us so that it appeared we were walking through an uninhabited country — uninhabited, except of course for the local fauna.

During the last mile of one cold December trek, when the frost was starting to crisp the grass and night seemed to be tugging at our collars, I heard a rustle from the trees behind me that stopped me in my tracks. My family tramped on, unaware, while I hesitantly turned round. Just for a moment or two, I was held by the sight of a skeletal wood clustered against an icy blue afterglow and the faint white snick of a new moon hanging above it. There was something else; a vague movement along the trees' edge, something running not quite soundlessly, yet very fast into deeper shadow where it vanished. Fox? Deer? Goblin? I had no idea, but then I was seven years old and all I had seen of the wild, apart from birds, were rabbits, red squirrels (this was 1955) and hedgehogs.

Despite the fact that an animal running for cover in the dark is an unremarkable event, what made it magical was its first-timeness and the way my senses, already sharpened by the half-light, almost convinced me I was leaping forward in pursuit of whatever it was. Being fearful, I never moved an inch, yet however brief the encounter it was a foretaste of what was to come when, less and less hesitantly, I began to venture out into the dark on my own. I discovered that the landscape had two lives: in the day there were birds and other fleetingly glimpsed creatures, but there were also people who disturbed the birds and made the earth-bound fauna disappear completely. At night there were no people anywhere, not even bogeymen; the only birds I saw were owls, but there were all kinds of other creatures, each one casually going about its night-time business, a whole secret world coming alive in the undisturbed dark. So I learnt not to make any disturbances myself, to creep like a mouse into a wood and sit still for maybe an hour, focusing with my ears, using the sounds of paw-patter or antler-click to colour in the invisible shapes until I could identify them or they came into shadowy view.

And if, later, I ever came across, say, a deer out in the open in broad daylight, it never had the same effect as when I glimpsed it moving under trees in dappled moonlight. In the daytime a deer or a fox only borrowed my eyes, but at night everything was stolen.

But now, at last light, because these words are fading like invisible ink into the greying page, I shall put down my pen, pull on my boots and see what this new night has in store for me.

3

Northward

It was almost ten thirty by the kitchen clock when I stepped out into the shadowy garden. Overhead, the velvet sky was about to release the first of a thousand stars while down at my feet the daisies, which all day had been gazing eagerly into the blue, were folded tight, like children hiding behind their hands from overwhelming relations.

The epic thrush had finally exhausted himself about half an hour earlier. Since then there had been silence, apart from the occasional bleating from ten-week-old lambs that, with their mothers, were settling down for the night under the twin oaks. When I took a few steps forward to get a better view into the west, where the twilight was still quite strong, I realized there was already a star – or, rather, a planet: Venus, almost lost in the glow, like a candle floating on a lake. A couple of bats flickered across it and a large moth swooped close to my face; the first signs that nightlife had begun.

The evening smelt as if the pores of the earth had opened to filter an underground river through all the acres of herb-rich grass around me. After the thin, dessicated atmosphere of the previous week, the humidity seemed almost tropical, and because sounds travel further in moist air I could clearly hear the last sleepy squawks from the rookery, even though they were from a copse a quarter of a mile away. The bats were probably sonaring somewhere above me, but I could not be certain. When I was a child, their ticking and squeaking were so obvious that I thought my parents must have gone deaf when, one evening when bats were skimming the eaves of a favourite wood, they told me they could not hear them; but later, in my mid-forties, my own children were perplexed to discover that I could no longer share the bat chatter with them – the high-frequency calls had, over a couple of summers, gone above my radar.

On a day when I just need a few re-energizing miles walking through varied country, I sometimes have to spin a coin to decide which path to follow. From home, I can set off towards any point of the compass, and every direction takes me through woods, across fields and over hills, but on a midsummer night I only ever head north.

This is high ground, with chalk escarpments ascending to over nine hundred feet; there is no light pollution, therefore, if the night is clear, the faint solar glare that slowly swings west–east along the northern horizon is always visible. Even a full moon, because it rides low to the south in June, cannot distract me from this guiding light.

Under any night sky, summer or winter, starlit or cloudy, no path is invisible once my eyes have adapted to the dark. Only when it dives under a thickly canopied wood will the path disappear completely, yet even then I never use a torch. Torchlight shows me precisely where to place my feet, but it blinds me to the world outside the bright tunnel of the beam. Amongst trees it can become a detonator, sending startled woodpigeons exploding through branches; and in the more open spaces it spotlights my presence to everything within miles. Furthermore, if I enter the disorienting blackness of truly dense woodland, I quite enjoy navigating through it, especially if my feet lose the feel of the path and the chinks of dim sky in the canopy are the only stars to steer by. But though I can even enjoy the occasional stab of primal fear in those darkest corners – my ancestral ghosts reminding me that night was once a dangerous place – what I like best is to slowly and meanderingly climb towards the glowing north edges of a June midnight. With each ridge or slope I approach, the glow defines the skyline, creating a new theatre for me to patiently scan, sometimes with binoculars, hoping to catch an episode of the nocturnal shadow play that is only visible during this short season.

Perhaps there will be a show, perhaps nothing at all. Having experienced plenty of blank nights during apparently promising conditions, I try to check my natural optimism. The entire landscape can seem devoid of life one night, pattering with activity the next. It is like casting into a promising pool but never

being quite sure when or if the fish will stir; yet sometimes even a dull fishing day will suddenly prickle with
expectation and my instinct will tell me that something
is definitely going to happen.

The air was not exactly prickling as I walked out of
the garden and into the adjacent copse, but I felt happy
and calm, and I crept through the already dark interior
without disturbing a single woodpigeon – always a
good early test. Instead of climbing the slope behind
the house I followed a path along the foot of it until the
trees gave way to steep open pasture.

Everything along the ridge above me was in solid
unillumined silhouette: a heart-shaped hawthorn, a
young ash tree, several clumps of thistle and at least
five pairs of rabbit ears. There is a warren on the edge
of the trees, so there was nothing special about night-
hopping bunnies; however, being small, they provided
useful focal points as I pre-adjusted my binoculars for
some hoped-for later encounter.

I was going to wait a few minutes for the rabbits to
nibble their way out of sight. They were only about forty
yards away; I did not want to scare them and cause
a ripple of panic that might alarm something more

interesting, yet in the twitch of an ear they all sat upright and alert with their heads turned to one side. Had there been a suspicious rustle in the grass? Fox? Weasel? I raised the binoculars again, scanning the ridge as an antlered deer head rose slowly above it and seemed to loom towards me. My low angle of vision and the halo of twilight made it appear not only larger than it was, but also slightly unreal – a mythic descendant from the time when all this was one vast medieval deer forest.

I blame the magical light, the intoxicating air and the 8x25 optics. It was just a roe buck, Britain's smallest native deer, but when I lowered the glasses I could still see it was a fine specimen, with impressive antlers. It stood on the ridge for just a few moments and seemed to be staring straight at me. I presumed it was going to utter its hell-hound bark and gallop away, scattering the rabbits, but slowly and rather mysteriously it simply backed out of sight, merging into the black skyline. Eager to see where it was heading, and sending the rabbits back down their burrows, I quickly climbed to the top of the slope where there was nothing but an empty sheep field. And not a sound. High to the north-east, the first stars gleamed at me.

4

Night Air

Hesitating a few moments at the edge of the sheep field, wondering whether to follow the north-western or northern route to the hills, I realized the night was not as silent as I first thought. My slightly huffy breath after running up the slope had drowned the sound of a different kind of breathing. When I first became aware of it I thought I was hearing the sound of water – maybe an overflowing sheep trough, but the cause became obvious as soon as I began walking towards it.

The wide sheep field is islanded with a number of beech clumps, each consisting of a tight group of tall, century-old trees. Every clump stood absolutely still under the first stars, except for one, which, as I could tell when I went up to it, was quivering restlessly in an isolated nocturnal breeze.

In the overall quiet the steady rustling was unexpected, but there was nothing strange happening. Especially when the sky is clear, the air can discover new forms of expression once the sun has set, particularly so in this rumpled landscape of high, grassy hills and deep, narrow valleys. As the air calms at the end of a summer day it begins to generate a subtle and complex interweaving of currents: cool air pouring down from the hilltops, warm air rising up the valley sides, a localized weather system of minor katabatic and anabatic winds that can, as in the sheep field, create interesting side effects. What surprised me was the strength of the breeze – certainly not a wind, but a fairly constant flow into the column of trees and yet not seemingly beyond them into a nearby wood; nor was there any sensation of moving air at ground level; only the upper halves of the trees were trembling.

I decided that, as I had already come halfway across the field, I might as well continue in that direction, heading north rather than following the north-western path back on the ridge. So, thanking the trees for pointing the way, I turned and began walking again; however, I had only gone a few yards when the rustling behind me stopped almost suddenly, the fade-out sounding just like a hosepipe being turned off. I paused in mid-step, expecting the breeze to rise again, but it had lost its energy completely or else, like me, had just wandered away along some new path.

The field curved gently downwards towards a fence-line where the ground fell steeply away into the next valley. There was still a touch of afterglow along the valley's upper slopes, while down below the darkness was broken here and there by the pale shapes of dozing sheep, like stepping stones in a black river. A tawny owl called from the copse on my right and I called back, hoping to tempt him out of his tree. Even a poor rendition of the call can convince an inquisitive or aggressive bird, especially in autumn and spring when the adult males are constantly rehooting their territory. And no matter how often I observe an owl's silent flight it always raises the pulse a little. There is something miraculous about the way the bird materializes out of a clear night sky – first a distant eclipsing of some faint star cluster then the gradually solidifying moth-like shape that sometimes passes just a yard over my head. (Remembering how the great bird photographer, Eric Hoskings, lost an eye to a tawny, I try not to tease an owl in an after-dark wood where it might be impossible to tell when or if I was being swooped at.) At this time of the year tawnys are usually mute, but there are always a few non-conformists, like the one in the copse – though as he didn't answer my call I presumed he was not interested in me. Yet perhaps he made a low fly-pass that I missed seeing, because a minute after my last warbling whistle there was a sudden alarm call of a blackbird trailing away from a nearby hawthorn. Owls hunt roosting birds as well as mice, but maybe the blackbird was more convinced by my call than the tawny.

The darkness of the valley was emphasized by the northerly radiance that it curved towards. The glow appeared too strong for the hour before midnight, yet it silhouetted only a relatively short stretch of skyline. The higher I looked the more stars I could see, and when I turned round the Milky Way was smeared all the way down to the south.

A nightwalk is not really the right description for my
nocturnal outings; they are more a random series of
stops, some of which last just a moment or two while
others continue for maybe an hour, depending on
whatever it is that has attracted my attention. My
conciousness of time is vague and mostly non-existent,
and the only concern I have about progressing towards
an objective is if I am late to see the sunrise from a
favourite vantage point or when a mirage of my teapot
urges me home.

I have no idea how long I stood watching the stars
grow brighter, but it was long enough to see two brilliant meteors, hear several large insects buzz overhead
like clockwork aeroplanes and feel the air begin to
change again. The faintest draught rising from the
valley feebled to nothing, leaving a still space for
another unexpected current. It came in across the field
on my left with a whisper but gusted past me like a
phantom bus. Stronger yet much more fleeting than
the sheep field breeze, it blew by along the fenceline
and flustered away into the distance.

Perhaps the new weather front coming in earlier
from the south had disrupted the normal flow of cool

air from the northerly hills, holding it back like a high tide reversing a river. But now the tide had turned for the night and the pent-up air had gone on a bit of a rampage.

Straightening my hat, I waited until everything calmed, then began walking again, descending into the valley, going slowly and carefully so as not to disturb the slumbering sheep.

5

A Circle in
the Grass

The path that runs along the length of the valley
inclines gently to the north and as I headed that way I
could feel a coolness flowing against me. The grass was
not exactly dew-soaked, but my boots swung through
it more quietly and easily than when I was crossing the
dry upper pasture. Tall trees along both slopes accentuated the valley's depth, increasing the sense of enclosure. Even when the trees began to thin out it was still
easy to imagine I was walking through a canyon.

Distances do not seem to obey the laws of perspective after dark. Though the high skyline ahead
was clearly visible, my path disappeared into general

darkness after only about ten yards. Despite my steady pace, the continually limited foreground plus a total lack of any middle distance eventually gave me the impression that I was either walking incredibly slowly or the hill beyond the valley's end, which had seemed so close, was actually a hundred miles away. As long as I kept looking straight ahead the illusion kept working, but then something broke the spell by kicking out of a tussock next to me and sweeping up the slope to my left. I knelt down to get a glimpse of it against the starry sky and saw a rapidly diminishing shape, long and low, yet with long legs – a startled hare that reached its vanishing point in an instant.

Carefully, I went over to where the animal had sprung from, thinking I might have disturbed a female with leverets. Details were obscure, even close to, but I eventually found an opened purse of grass blades that was warm and dry when I pressed my palm into it. There were, however, no infants.

It would have been unusual, though not unheard of, to find a doe with young so close to a footpath.

A few years ago, my son Will discovered a form containing three new-born leverets by the path that crosses the sheep field, and, more recently, I watched a hare making a round-about approach to her nursery just a stone's throw from our house. I was looking out of my window on a late May evening when I saw her appear from under the oaks and lollop slowly round in a wide half-circle across the field. For a minute or two she paused, sitting calmly in the long grass with her ears at half-cock, before trotting forward again and eventually completing the circuit. After another short interval, she began to run slightly faster, her course now describing a gradually tightening spiral, her pace quickening and her ears flat as she wheeled round and round towards the centre, as if she had been caught up in a mysterious vortex. Finally she stopped and slowly sank down out of sight into the grass. I kept my eyes fixed on the spot, but night came on and she did not reappear.

Hares may act eccentrically at times; I have watched them boxing, chasing and somersaulting, yet I have never seen that kind of behaviour before. I presumed it was defensive, an instinctive strategy for preventing a direct approach from a predator that might have picked up her scent. By leading, say, a fox in a circle around her she would have plenty of time to hear or smell it coming and run, drawing it away from the leverets before accelerating and leaving it in a cloud of grass pollen. And I am convinced she was nursing young because, over the next two evenings, I saw her either returning to or reappearing from the same place. Whether coming or going, she repeated the dizzy routine, spiralling inward or outward, and whenever she went beyond the field's boundary I was tempted to sneak through the grass, just to confirm that youngsters were at home. But I decided to leave them in peace.

Until the mid 1960s, *Lepus* used to make an occasional appearance near my childhood home on the North Downs. If I saw it running across an open stretch of grassland it always popped my eyes. Even when cantering with its long ears erect, a hare moves with an easy grace, but when it suddenly drives forward, with its ears swept back and its stride longer than its long body, it seems to be flying rather than running. That image, which made such a powerful impression on me when I was young, became increasingly rare as the hare's territory was either ravaged or continually disturbed, and by the time I left that landscape, in the 1970s, I had not seen it for years.

A Circle in the Grass

Where I walk nowadays, two counties westwards, the downland is far less tramelled and the brown hare is not uncommon, yet there are fewer than there were twenty years ago and so I try not to disturb them. However, if I see one in the distance, quietly feeding, usually in the evening, I am often tempted to call it. A hare is an inquisitive creature; if it hears the squealing of one of its kind, which is fairly easy to imitate, I can often persuade it to investigate. As long as I never move once I have the hare's attention it will, hesitantly, begin to approach. Several times I have managed to intrigue an animal to within a few feet of me. During one very close encounter, as I 'called' while sitting back against a fencepost, a hare that seemed almost the size of a roe deer reared up onto its hind legs and raised its head so that we were looking at each other eye to eye – and what strange high-set eyes they were, staring with a terrible intensity, expressing something much wilder and stranger than I could imagine. I was no threat to it because I remained absolutely motionless, and it looked at me as if I were not really there, or as if I were a conundrum that made no sense. After an electric half minute, it went down onto its forepaws, twitched its whiskers and unhurriedly loped away across a field.

When my daughter Camilla was two years old I drew her a picture of a leaping hare and she immediately asked, or rather demanded, that I introduce her to a real one. It was springtime, when the animals are at their most active, and we walked to a field where I had often seen them playing and feeding. As we approached the field's edge I picked Camilla up so that we made just one suspicious shape rather than two. We spotted a hare almost straight away. It was sitting quietly on its own, about seventy yards away, and it turned to face us as soon as I began to squeak at it. After a moment it trotted towards us quite quickly until, just a few paces away, it stopped, sat upright and stared.

'What big ears it has!' I whispered. 'And look at its lovely eyes!'

But then I realized my little girl was not looking. She had been watching as the hare approached, but when it stared at us she covered her face with her hands.

'Eyes!' she said. 'Don't want to see 'em!'

In the valley, not long before midnight, as I set off along the footpath again, I remembered those eyes and felt they were still watching me.

6

THE HALF-HEARD BIRD

This landscape is not wild, but its geography and history have preserved its sense of remoteness; and it is quiet, sometimes very quiet. During the high moons of December I regularly walk a few miles before bed, but whenever I stop and listen out for nightlife all I usually hear is my own pulse. In cold, clear conditions, when the frost lies silvery on the fields, these valleys and hollows become like fine glass bowls that tremble at the slightest whisper. Sometimes the silence is threatened by the needling call of a night-flying redwing or the faint patter of fox paws, and sometimes I hear the burble of a diesel train, seven miles to the north. On summer nights, despite the fact that every distant sound is muffled by the density of foliage, there is never such depth to the quiet.

As I continued walking, the valley seemed soundless, but when I paused for a moment, because I thought I heard an unexpected birdcall, I realized I was surrounded by noise, albeit muted noise. The ground below a solitary oak tree to my right was alive with minuscule scrapings and clickings as nocturnal insects worked through a scattering of dead leaves. The tiny vibrations were interrupted by a rodent – probably a vole – as it twitched between the grass blades at my feet, but then this rustling became, in turn, overlaid by the contented munching of a midnight-feasting sheep, just visible on the right-hand slope. From the near distance, fledgling owls kept up a constant background of mono- tonous wheezing and squeaking. The sound I had stopped to hear, the half-heard bird, was not repeated, though I replayed it in my head and tried to match it to a species. It had come from high overhead – a faint, thin, descending glissando, not unlike the redwing's call in winter, yet more sustained, a bit like the cry of a lapwing. Maybe it was the sound of a falling star; maybe I had imagined it. I started walking again and immediately all the little noises became completely inaudible, overwhelmed by the sound of my footsteps in the grass and the soft friction of oncoming air across my ears.

Where there had been a few solitary trees on the slopes there were now dark woods crowding in on both sides, converging as I approached the valley's end, but allowing me to pass between them. My path led to a crossway. Ahead, it continued up a rounded grassy hillock, a place known locally as Quaking Grass Hill; to the left a track led between trees towards a narrow secluded valley, while to the right it curved north-eastward through woods towards a high escarpment. The small dark hill in front of me rose up out of dark woods and curved across the much less dark northern sky. Because, on previous nights, I had often seen the silhouettes of animals crossing the open slope I lingered a few moments at the crossway, but soon noticed that the grass above me was beginning to glow with a grey light. Over some other hill to the east, out of sight from my low position, the moon had obviously just risen, an event as predictable and ordinary as the swing of a clock hand. Yet no matter how many hundreds I have seen in the past, a moonrise is always like a new discovery to me. Every night, as long as the sky is clear, it appears differently according to its phase, though when new it does not, of course, appear at all. Less magnificent than a sunrise, but more enchanting, a moonrise is irresistible, and so, disregarding the nightlife potential, I headed up the slope to watch the illuminations.

The moon was behind me as I climbed. When I finally looked round it was much higher in the sky than I had expected and silver rather than gold. A waning gibous, about a week after full, it was not quite big enough to dazzle, yet as it floated higher the interior of the valley below filled with a blueish mist, the lunar glow lighting up a layer of moist air, like someone breathing on cold glass.

I was not the only daytime creature admiring the lightshow. From the edge of the trees to my left, a woodpigeon began to coo, repeating his familiar soft-toned mantra – a mesmerizing sound in that setting, though not unique for I have often heard pigeons serenading the moon. Lacking the critical judgement of, say, a wren, they are probably deceived into thinking a new day is dawning. But the new day was still several hours away.

THE HALF-HEARD BIRD

Eventually the insomniac bird fell silent and the only sound was the crunching of an apple. The grass was drier on the hill than in the valley and I had settled down to take some refreshment. In the capacious pockets of my jacket I also had a flapjack, a packet of crisps, a bottle of water and a banana. Normally I only take an apple. The one I ate was perfect for the time of night – crisp and not too sweet – and I munched it down to the pips. But apples are the noisiest fruit and the silence seemed absolute when it was finished. Only gradually did I begin to detect distant sounds again: something scuffling through the undergrowth in the woods, the squeaking owlets and then, as I was about to begin walking once more, the same birdcall that had mystified me before. It seemed to come from the height of the stars – a brief, ultra-fine *keeeee* – but it was clearer this time and I think it was a swift.

Long before I read that swifts can remain airborne for the first two or three years of their life, flying day and night, I knew they had owlish habits. Back in the early 1970s, when I used to fish a large disused gravel pit in Surrey, my June evenings would sometimes fill with countless numbers of swifts, more than I had ever seen at a single location before or since. The myriad of crescent wings would sweep low across the water at sunset, sometimes skimming the surface, and every few minutes a group of them would utter their piercing signature scream. As the afterglow faded those birds that did not head back to the nest sites continued to wheel higher and higher, the flock eventually smudging into the darkening sky hundreds of feet above me. And long after the first stars had appeared I would still catch the occasional high-altitude call, like the one I thought I heard above the hill. As dawn approached the swifts would silently reappear, flying low across the water again, but only in small groups, as if their nocturnal flight – in which they must have slept – had scattered them across the sky. Only at sunrise, almost two hours after first light, were the birds congregating in large numbers again.

Since that time, forty years ago, I had not heard the night call of the swift again; and because I only ever see small groups of them nowadays it seems unlikely that what I heard at midnight really was a swift. To properly identify it I needed to hear it a third time and so I sat back down in the grass for a few more minutes, listening to the quiet sky.

7

FIRST SIGHT

Named after a distinctive downland plant whose delicate flowers quiver in the softest breeze, Quaking Grass
Hill – my midnight vantage point – was a much-loved
place with my children when they were young. They
would play hide and seek, crawling between knee-high
tussocks and boulder-sized anthills, or they would roll
or flap their arms and fly down the slope. In spring and
early summer they had to play more carefully in case
they disturbed a skylark or some other ground-nesting
bird, but by creeping watchfully they discovered all
kinds of other things that might have been missed:
spiral-patterned snails, great tank-like beetles, vividly

marked caterpillars, sulphur yellow butterflies, shrews, grasshoppers and, always a favourite, slow worms, weaving their gold coils through the grass blades like eels gliding between lily stems.

Wherever it happened and whatever the creature, with each first encounter there was always a moment's pause for the little shock of revelation, a sudden sharpening of vision that said yes, this really is something different. A new discovery added a new colour to a world that might have seemed less brilliant had my tribe not delved or squelched or splashed so eagerly into it, but only the two eldest developed their own special interests. Camilla was an avid bug hunter, a five-year-old entomologist who once brought home a magnificent specimen of *Timarcha tenchricosa*, the bloody-nosed beetle, which she kept for a few days in a leaf-filled goldfish bowl before releasing it into the wild again. A spider that sat down beside her always received her full attention and she was delighted to conduct a leg count on a centipede or spot check a ladybird.

When he was six, Alex became obsessed by lizards after the first sight of a common lizard as it zipped into a bramble thicket while we were out for a walk. As soon as we got home that day he needed to see a picture of one and I had several examples in my collection of nature books; but such was his enthusiasm I had to buy him his own copy of *Reptiles and Amphibians of Europe* the next time we went into a book shop. The following night I found him fast asleep, using the book as a pillow, his head resting on a full-page illustration of the beloved lizard; and the day after, as we were driving across Salisbury Plain, thirty miles from home, a common lizard ran across the road in front of us, something that, as far as I'm aware, had never happened before or has since. It was as if Alex had magicked it.

I understood his passion as the same kind of fever had afflicted me when I was his age. Despite being aware of the shadowy presence of foxes and deer in the nearby woods, as a sapling I had no idea there were reptiles living on our local heath, though I must have unknowingly disturbed several whenever I galloped through the bracken with my cowboy and Indian friends. My parents were not actively interested in natural history; despite their fondness for long-distance walking through remote countryside their main intererests were music, books and left-wing politics. Therefore, while I enjoyed my father playing the piano music of his favourite composers, Bach and Bartok, while my mother would read me children's stories from round the world and while I was familiar with all the neighbourhood socialists and communists, I knew no one who could tell me about the local wildlife. But then I met an amateur snake charmer.

Tori de Souza lived in Columbo, Sri Lanka, or Ceylon as we called it then. He was, I think, the editor of the *Times of Ceylon*, whom my father had met and befriended while retreating from the Japanese during the Second World War. Tori sailed over to visit us in 1954 and after he and father had caught up on a decade's news he began to relate stories about his far-away land, describing a vast jungle north of his home and the snake charmers who would sometimes emerge from it. For a few coins, they would conjure cobras out of baskets by playing on a flute and Tori whistled a rendition of one of their sinuous melodies. As he did so he took a small basket out of his pocket and, with a flourish, placed it on the table in front of us. Nothing happened, so he told my sister Helen, my brother Nick and me to keep our heads down with just our eyes peeping over the edge of the table. He whistled again and, very slowly, a small green snake raised its head from the basket. For a moment I was convinced it was real, but I saw my big sister smile a knowing smile and, afterwards, only the infant Nick remained wide-eyed. Yet I still thought it a wonderful trick — an inflatable plastic serpent connected by a thin tube to a rubber bulb in Tori's pocket. Despite the fakery, Tori said that snakes really did respond to music's vibrations, and as it was a perfect day for a snake hunt perhaps he could prove it.

Because of the pictures in our *Children's Encyclopaedia* I knew there was nothing as exciting as a cobra in England, but there were grass snakes, adders and smooth snakes, which sounded just as exotic. We went for a walk over the heath, where Tori found a thorny, tangled place that reminded him of a proper jungle. He began warbling the snake charm again, and having recently learned how to whistle myself I was allowed to add an impromptu accompaniment. No snake appeared so we dutifully whistled the charm over another likely spot and after a moment's tense expectation Tori suddenly held his hand up, signalling silence. We three children stood still and mute, staring at the gorse and brambles in front of us.

'Listen!' whispered Tori. Was there a snake hissing or was it the breeze? Was there a serpent crawling towards us or was that the breeze, too? Because we were listening and imagining so intently we were certain the undergrowth was alive with stealthy sounds, though we did not, of course, see an actual snake. Nevertheless, I was convinced enough to repeat the charm whenever I went back to the heath on my own and found a promising-looking thicket. And because dense scrub is an ideal habitat for many kinds of small animal, I frequently heard what I believed were secretive responses to the whistle. My greatest success was when a rabbit popped out of a hole in a hedge, but I don't know who was more surprised or disappointed. No snake ever materialized, but it didn't really matter because my searching finally led me to an equally lovely member of the reptile family.

Towards the end of that same summer Helen joined me in another snake hunt across the heath. As we worked through an acre of heather I spied a small brightness in the purple flowers at my feet and stopped to share a few seconds with an astonishing creature – a slender golden-coloured lizard with sepia stripes running from head to tail and bold flecked markings along the velvety-looking flanks. Though not much larger than the newts I sometimes saw in a nearby field pond, it had far more *presence* than a mere amphibian. Helen was a few yards to my right and I whispered her over to me just as it slipped away into the heather. My first sight of *Lacerta vivapira* was the key to a vast lizard domain that had been somehow hidden from me until then. Over subsequent summers, as I learnt to identify the favoured basking places, I beheld many similar jewel-like apparitions, sometimes two or three together, some more beautifully coloured than others, some more vividly marked.

In the same way that the village pond had been transformed from a big splashy puddle to a haunt of monsters once I discovered the reality of carp, so the heathland became less of a playground and more a location for genuine adventure now I had stumbled on its secret life. But in all the years I hunted quietly through the bracken and heather, though I saw scores of lizards, and caught a few, I never once saw a snake, and because of that I began to get as mad about them as Alex was – and still is – about lizards.

8

STALKER

There were no more birdcalls from above, though there were a few more soporific and confused woodpigeons cooing to the moon from the trees below. Had my ears been as sensitive as they were a few decades ago I would, perhaps, also have heard the bats as they flick-ered back and forth across the pale sky. I suppose I had been sitting on the side of the hill for about twenty minutes, watching the bats, listening to the night. Though the air was cool I was not cold. A clear night in June can be as cold as an overcast night in December, so unless the weather is sultry I usually wear a padded jacket, with gloves and scarf in my pockets for the chilly hour before dawn. However, I was still warm from the previous hours' walking, and rather too comfortable; in fact I had just decided to pull my hat down, lie back and have a doze when I heard the slightest sound – a sound like a finger pressing into dry grass – right behind me.

Two conflicting impulses vied for control: instinctive and rational. In the split second before I slowly turned my head I tried to persuade myself not to because this sneaky behaviour was familiar to me and I was certain I knew the culprit. It would, therefore, surely be more interesting to remain motionless and let the sneak reveal itself quietly; but the primal auto-alarm of skin prickle and blood fizz made stillness unthinkable. So I turned and came face to face with the image I had expected to see – another roe deer. It had crept up quietly through tall grass and I had been completely unaware until I heard that delicate hoof-step when it was almost in touching distance. For a moment we stared at one another, both weighing up the situation. The deer was obviously unhappy with me because it suddenly bellowed a ferocious bark, leapt backwards and bounded away over the hill. The bark seemed to echo for a long time, but not as long as it took for my heart rate to slow down. While I am familiar with the surprising strength of a roe buck's voice, I have never had one bark in my face before.

Despite roe deer being mostly shy, evasive creatures, the bucks are often overcome by curiosity, possibly aggressive curiosity, as a result of territorial concerns or maybe just natural inquisitiveness. I do not think I have ever experienced a display of overt aggression, the bark signifying alarm rather than anger, but I have often been stalked by this goat-sized animal. The last time it happened I was lying in the hayfield above the house watching a meteor shower when I glimpsed a deer's vague silhouette approaching silently from my left. I managed to remain still and it came to within a few feet before turning and galloping off into the dark. Three summers ago, I was asleep on a reedy lake bank waiting for a carp when I jolted awake to find a deer standing directly over me. One second it was there, the next it was gone.

Only infrequently have I been deer-stalked in daylight and only once when I was moving – walking through long grass with a roe buck following thirty or so yards behind. When I entered a wood, the deer stopped and stared after me for several minutes before turning and trotting breezily away.

Other deer types do not, in my experience, behave in the same way, although I often see fallow and some of the more recently introduced species. Perhaps this is because roe deer lead a mostly solitary life and therefore, instead of following a herd they have more time to follow a whim. However, despite not sensing any aggression, I am sometimes a little wary because I remember the animal behaviourist, Konrad Lorenz, writing about how the roe buck 'is about the most malevolent beast I know'. He was describing captive deer in large enclosures, but while he said that the animal was generally considered to be 'second only to the dove in the proverbial gentleness of its nature' he warned that, in reality, it was 'a ruthless and blood-thirsty murderer ... and is possessed, into the bargain, with a weapon, its antlers, which it shows mighty little restraint in putting into use'.

Lorenz had observed the same kind of slow, stealthy approach that I've just experienced, but his buck was sneaking up to a doe and its young, inching right next to them before lowering its head and goring both to death. He then went on to say how, in the roe buck's enclosure, an uninitiated person would not recognize this slow approach as an 'earnest attack', which gave rise to the fact that, in Lorenz's time, there were more serious accidents caused by 'tame' deer than captive lions and tigers.

Wild roe deer are obviously far more nervous of humans than captive specimens, and I have never heard of anyone being assaulted by one, but the next time I stop to contemplate the moon I shall try to keep Lorenz's words in mind while remembering to watch my back.

9

INTO THE TREES

On the eastern slope of Quaking Grass Hill is a strip of ancient woodland, a remnant of a once great forest that, until the clearances of a few centuries ago, had shaded these valleys for thousands of years. Every spring I like to visit it simply to breathe its air, which, at that time, is layered with alternate lungfuls of sweet bluebell and pungent wild garlic. Last night, when I stepped through the outer branches, all I could smell was the faintly honeyed perfume of the trees. The bluebells and ransome flowers have died back and nothing else will bloom now that the canopy overhead is complete. Earlier in the year, when the boughs were still leafless, there were celandines and primroses, anemones and violets, but now, apart from the pale plumes of tooth-wort, there will be no relief to the overall green and brown until the yellow leaves fall in autumn.

The colourless midnight wood had the same stored-up warmth and hushed boxed-in quiet as an old high-raftered barn – quiet, but not soundless. The interior of any summer wood after dark is nearly always gently clicking, rustling, pattering and squeaking as the mostly small creatures busy themselves with their nocturnal routines. Sometimes there are unlocatable rufflings as birds fluster their wings in sleep, and if the previous day has been hot there might be the occa-sional quite sharp crack or creak of cooling dead wood. Even the tiniest mouse-tremble is accentuated in the enclosed resonant space, which makes a patrolling badger sound like a trundling bear.

Before I began picking my way towards the wood's centre I paused for a moment to accustom myself to the more intense darkness. There was nothing to see but a few spots of moonlight glowing on the branches and trunks in front of me, nor was there much to hear except for a curious, subdued tap-tapping that sounded like something patiently hammering at a root, though I could not imagine what animal might be responsible. As soon as I stepped forward the sound was drowned by the clattering of a pigeon's wings, the bird panicking through the canopy and flapping noisily away. A twig snapping underfoot had spooked the pigeon; the pigeon had silenced the tapping. I took more care afterwards, feeling rather than seeing my way through or over the various almost invisible obstacles, making slow, hesitant progress towards my objective. Though I'd not intended to detour into the trees, the hours under the open sky had made the idea more appealing; and anyway, night or day, however much I appreciate the optimistic sweep and spaciousness of downland, I can never resist the intimate atmosphere of a wood.

The impressions formed in my childhood, when every sense except common sense was razor sharp, marked the path I was destined to follow, a path that still constantly bends towards what my child's eye regarded as the two most important elements in the world: the woody and the watery. From my earliest days, if there was no pond or stream to splash into, I would be just as happy plunging into trees.

Amongst friends, a wood could be many different things: a castle, a dragon's lair, an Indian camp, a hideout; but when I was alone it was just itself – an enclosed, secretive space with unusual light and its own distinctive personality. There were also signs that the local woods were alive in a way that the surrounding fields were not. Because of the network of strange little paths that criss-crossed through undergrowth often too dense even for a six-year-old, I knew that the trees were concealing some kind of curious activity. At first I wondered whether the tracks had been made by the same kinds of beings depicted in my favourite books, but were they friendly, like elves, or did they have a darker intent, like witches? This half-magical, half-sinister quality was characteristic of other places I loved, particularly the aforementioned village pond where I had discovered monsters, *real* monsters; but a wood offered escape as well as mystery and, especially on a breezy summer day, I could voyage halfway round the world under the sails of the trees.

The paths were a puzzle, though, and I kept going back to them, hoping to discover the identity of the pathmakers. If only I'd been more determined to push through the undergrowth I might eventually have stumbled on a badger sett or fox earth, but thorns and timidness prevented me, and in the absence of any knowledgable guide I remained ignorant of the facts. However, according to the stories in my books, all woodland paths were unreliable because trees could alter their positions after dark, confusing any traveller stupid enough to be out at that time. The trees were in league with the wood's inhabitants, who would appear when the traveller was properly lost – and some of them were cruel. Sitting at home with a picture book I knew this idea was a fantasy, but if I was anywhere near the woods when the light faded in the evening I knew it was true.

While the paths kept their secret until I was a few years older, the trees themselves were more forthcoming. The life that depended on them revealed itself as soon as I took a closer look: rabbit burrows between the roots, songbird's nests in the ivy round the trunks, woodpeckers or owls in the hollows, beetles and caterpillars on the bark and leaves, squirrel drays or crows' nests in the topmost branches. Whenever it rained, dozens of snails would materialize at the foot of each tree and, like magic marbles, inch vertically upwards towards the outspreading boughs. There were also a few individual trees that stood out from their companions because they were more venerable or more towering or seemed to radiate a kind of benevolence. One of these was an old yew with a great barrel of a trunk and densely layered boughs that I could climb almost like stairs, emerging finally on a roof so secure I could lie down as if on a mattress. I told some friends about it and we made a camp beneath the dome-like canopy, hanging important trophies from the branches and leaving them there as a sign of ownership, things like a box of comics, a plastic telescope and a pop gun. We had a daring plan to spend a night there, but even before we realized that none of us were really daring enough, our possessions vanished, taken by persons or creatures unknown, after which we never visited the tree again.

A whole forest of these remembered trees sprang up when I stepped under the branches last night, and I think my childhood self would have been impressed when, after a slow and uneventful walk through the blackness, I arrived at a slightly less than dark clearing, in the centre of which stood an ancient English oak. I knew it well, having discovered it back in the 1980s when I first explored these hills, and though I normally visit it in daylight, it seems so much more wondrous at night. It must have sprouted from its acorn at least six centuries ago and despite its unexceptional height and spread it has a massive girth. The east face of the trunk is so deeply grooved and contorted with age that, in daylight, it looks like a spiral of entwined crocodiles, while the west face is completely covered in moss and reminds me of a baggy green sofa. None of these features were visible in the dark because the half moon was too low to the south to penetrate the clearing and the great tree was lit only by the stars, but its massive presence was even more imposing than in sunlight. Standing below it, I could easily understand why the pagans invested such enduring and powerful beings with god-like qualities, and I suppose that perception – innocent, unclouded and reverent – was exactly how I viewed the world when I was a child. We were all pagans once, before we went to school.

10

The Ghost of
the Nightingale

Standing under the oak, thinking about the clouds of leaves that had unfurled overhead spring after spring to wither and fall autumn after autumn, I wondered how much longer it would endure. It has withstood over half a millennium of weather, survived drought and disease, avoided the axe and, more recently, the chainsaw; in its lifetime it has been a source of food and shelter for millions of birds, mammals and insects; it has witnessed countless changes: many neighbouring trees have died of old age or succumbed to other travails, some fine woods have been felled nearby, much of the surrounding downland has been ploughed, yet the landscape itself is probably as quiet as when the oak was a sapling; and at night in early summer the oak wood and all the other woods in the vicinity are even quieter now that the nightingales no longer return.

Midsummer would usually be too late, anyway, to hear a night song, whether the birds were present or not, but in their normal breeding season, from April to early June, their calls unfailingly echoed through the dark.

Comparing the nightingale with a blackbird, as I did yesterday evening, I was disparaging, yet though its song is not as inventive or as musical as the blackbird's, in the right setting it can be even more seductive. In the past – the long ago past – I have heard it in over-grown country gardens, on heathland, along hedged-in lanes, by rivers and lakes, in thorny wasteground bordering building and industrial sites and, once, at the end of a busy, illuminated airport runway. Each location's ambience varied the song's effect – the runway, for instance, making it seem heroically defiant. But the place that transformed it from birdsong into something not quite earthly – not quite heavenly, either – was an oak wood.

Three miles from the ancient tree is another fragment of old forest, twenty acres of trees, where, every spring, the nightingales would sing day and night until the dog rose blossomed. When the children were young their mother and I would sometimes take them to the wood on a fine May evening and listen to all the different songbirds gradually withdraw one by one until there were only the nightingales. They always sounded more joyful if the weather was benign, yet it was when most of them were subdued by the creeping onset of a storm that I heard the song at its best.

I went out alone after dark, curious to hear the contrasting mix of nightingale and distant thunder, though when I entered the wood all I could hear was a muffled cheeping that sounded like a bird whistling in a bag. An invisible path led me towards a familiar circle of oaks where, after a faint bass throb of thunder, a second nightingale struck up a more liquid yet equally half-hearted call, the dribbling notes dying as soon as I stepped into the clearing. I sat down in the grass, waited patiently and eventually the call was repeated — just as feebly. The bird was low down to my left, deep in a hazel bush, but when he unexpectedly recovered his voice he was everywhere.

A nightingale does not really sing, he chants, making a series of declamations in the manner of a thrush, though less stridently. In tones as cool and clear as springwater he voices elegies rather than halleluias. Once he began chanting, the bird in the clearing did not depart from the standard repertoire, yet there were slight variations to the formal phrasing: not only were his opening high-pitched notes extended for longer than usual, the typical bubbling chuckle began quite harshly, like the alarm cry of a blackbird, but then rippled gently into the succeeding, smoothly descending scale. The continued repetition of sparkling trills, fluid loops and shimmering undertones gradually built into something like the momentary singing deafness when the ears have been overwhelmed by noise. Not that the nightingale, just seven or eight yards away, was loud; but the dense night and the echoing ring of trees sharpened the edges of his voice, giving it a brightness that was sometimes dazzling.

In May 1975, in a cabin on the edge of an immense islanded lake in northern Poland, I was lullabied by a massed choir of nightingales that was still singing when I woke at sunrise, yet even that ocean of sound was not as magical or as impressive as the bird in our nearby oak wood. However, over the last decade the nightingales have gradually abandoned every wood, copse, thicket and spinney in the locality. Apart from the fact that the hazel is not coppiced as thoroughly as it used to be, nothing has happened to the bird's habitat to make them turn their beaks up at it, so I presume their absence must be due either to misfortunes at the African end of their migration or during the flight. I read recently that nightingale pâté has become a very fashionable delicacy in certain expensive European restaraunts. And because the lovely bird can now be sold for seven euros a smear there is no telling how many mist nets are being stretched across its migration route.

I once recorded a nightingale on a cheap Dictaphone, and by playing it back on a night when the birds were being sullen I would often provoke a competitive male to respond in song. But now, if I play the tape in the woods, hoping the birds might have returned, there is never any answering call. The thin, hazy sound of the recording has become like a faded memory, or a ghost.

11

A FEARFUL TALE

There is a deer track that runs the length of the wood, although it's hard to find on a summer night. In winter, when the trees and ground are bare and the moon is high, it is clearly visible, but last night it was only a suggestion of a crease in the dark clutter of vegetation. It led away from the clearing by the old tree and I felt my way along its winding course through the blackness. A deer track is easier to negotiate in the dark than a tunnelling badger run, yet deer slip through a tangled wood like fish through reeds, while a human can only creep like a beetle in long grass. Stepping carefully whenever my feet brushed roots or fallen branches I at least managed to avoid disturbing the wood pigeons, but something scampered away from me as I weaved through a hazel clump, running lightly and fast over the ground cover – almost certainly a fox. It was completely invisible and it reminded me that it wasn't so long ago – just eight years, to be precise – when such a blind encounter could, for the first time since I was a boy, unnerve me. Over a period of several months the night, the English night, began to feel as stealthy as it must have been when wolves and bears roamed the forests – and all because of a rumour.

It began on a summer morning when, in the wing mirror of his van, our postman, Rob, glimpsed what appeared to be a large black cat crossing the narrow road behind him. He described the sighting while delivering my letters and I was intrigued, especially as Rob is a sharply observant countryman with a wide knowledge of the local fauna. However, because the mirrored image lasted less than a second he could only say it *might* have been a cat. A few days later, Steve, Camilla's boyfriend at that time, who was unaware of Rob's story, was driving along the same stretch of road, between a copse and a high hedge, when something crossed in front of him. It was early morning, the low sun was in his eyes, but he said the creature was black and stocky, had a long thick tail and looked like a big cat.

Like the monster myths surrounding half the waters I've ever fished, big cat stories are not unusual nowadays. Ever since the Dangerous Animals Act of 1976, when it became illegal to keep pets like lions, wolves and puff adders, legends have grown around the possibility that not all the exotica were surrendered to the authorities, but released into the countryside instead. However, most of the sightings of big cats have been unconvincing, and of the dozens of photographs and video clips offered as evidence not many raise an eyebrow. A photo of an average domestic cat can look quite impressive if the moggie has nothing to scale it against and is silhouetted against the sun, but careful inspection will usually reveal details that give it away, and not necessarily the bell on the collar. As a nation, though, we love our legends, even if most of their subjects, like the Loch Ness Monster, can only exist in our imaginations. But now we had a local sighting, our own big cat story, like the Surrey Puma or the Beast of

Bodmin, and, despite my scepticism – though I didn't doubt the witnesses' sincerity – I felt I should at least do it the courtesy of further investigation.

One evening, I had a walk along the road with Alex and Will, both teenagers at that time, to inspect the cat's crossing. Apart from the small copse and hedgerows there was nothing that would have appealed to a large feline, and, surely, it would not have ventured across the surrounding wheat fields in daylight. It was, anyway, over a week since the sightings, long enough for any wandering cat to be at the other end of the country. The copse was a clump of poplars round a dried-up pond, and the moment we stepped between the trees we were startled by the sound of a fleeing animal. It might have been a fox or a roe deer or possibly a hare – the deep shadow made it impossible to tell. The fact that we had disturbed *something* was encouraging and we rushed out of the trees on the field side, hoping to see a movement in the acres of wheat, but nothing even quivered. We waited till it was almost dark, then walked home, unconvinced that we'd disturbed anything unusual, although reluctant to dismiss the possibility.

About a month later, again in the evening, Alex and a couple of his pals were walking home from a neighbouring village when they spotted a dark-looking animal lying in the grassy field they were about to cross. It was around two hundred yards away, and as they paused it stood up and padded slowly off into the woods on the far side. They circled back a different way and came home along the road, eager to tell me what they'd seen.

But what had they seen? And what had Rob and Steve seen? Was it a big cat, like a melanistic puma? Or was it just an oversize feral moggie or a feline-looking black dog? I asked some of the local gamekeepers and farmers if they had spotted anything similar stalking across their land, but apart from a black fox and a black fallow deer, both remembered from some years previously, there was nothing worth mentioning. And if there *were* a big cat – a possibly dangerous predator – how long would it be before someone had a close encounter with it?

I have a friend, Hugh, who is quite knowledgable on this subject, having spent many years focusing on different species of big cats through the lens of his film camera. Indeed, I think he has filmed, for television, *every* species of large feline on Earth, including the snow leopard, and all of them in their natural habitat. I asked him if he believed that such animals might be living wild in Britain, and, if so, was it possible that one of them could have made its territory in our neck of the woods? Yes and yes was his reply, though he was dismissive of the majority of reported sightings, offering his own next-door neighbour as the perfect example of an unreliable witness. The man was convinced he'd seen a big cat in the trees on the edge of his garden.

'It was a tiger!' laughed Hugh – meaning it was Tiger, Hugh's own quite large tabby.

However, he was certain that he himself had been in the presence of a genuinely outsize cat by a lake in Gloucestershire, ten years ago. He had not seen it, but after a lifetime stalking all kinds of predators and sometimes being stalked by them he had absolute faith in a familiar instinctive red-alert that warned him when a big cat was watching him. It was, he agreed, astonishing that he should have had that sense in the middle of the English countryside, yet the next day it was confirmed by a local keeper that a large, unidentified feline had, over the previous months, been spotted several times in the area.

Using a camera instead of a gun, Hugh is one of the world's most experienced hunters, but, after our conversation, as I set out for another evening walk through my local woods, I felt the same uneasiness I used to suffer as a child, venturing out in the dark after reading a ghost story. Unlike spooky tales, though, our cat story might well, as Hugh had said, turn out to be true, and that possibility gave an undeniably raw edge to the atmosphere. Despite rational arguments, I could not stay in the trees after dark, no matter how many nightingales may have tempted me.

Apart from the suspicious death of a sheep, the summer ended with nothing to add to the tale, but towards the middle of autumn, when my evening strolls had just begun to extend into the darkness again, Camilla, my eldest daughter, had a serious confrontation. She was on her way back from work, riding her bicycle in the dark, taking a short cut down a wooded track that led to the homeward road. Through the last few trees she saw a car speeding along the road, its headlights suddenly illuminating a large animal that dashed across the beams and continued running straight towards her. Five minutes later, when the front door burst open, Camilla's eyes seemed to come in before she did.

'I've just seen it!' she gasped.

The car had driven on without even slowing down, but in the not very bright light of her bike lamp Camilla watched the embodiment of the local rumour sprint past her. They were so close they had almost collided. It was black, she said, and as thick-backed as the jaguar we once saw at a zoo when she was a little girl. As it vanished up the track, she swerved onto the road and pedalled frantically home. Had she been unaware of the rumour it would still have been a hair-raising experience; under the circumstances it was, in its English pastoral setting, just as terrifying as one of Hugh's 'dodgy moments', like when a man-eating tiger stalked him in a Bangladeshi jungle. However, never easily spooked and resilient by nature, Camilla soon stopped trembling, reasoning, over a cup of tea, that having just dodged a car the animal had probably been more frightened than her.

So we really *did* have a big cat living in the woods, or at least we thought we did, but the following spring our supposedly identified species was metaphorically shot full of holes. Andy, an ex-keeper who lives in a cottage less than a mile from us, has spent every working day of his life in this landscape and when I told him our story he was naturally interested – but he was not convinced. While he believed that six different people had definitely seen a large black animal, he was also fairly certain it was a dog. Close to where Rob and Steve had spotted something running across the road is a farm, home to an old, overweight black Labrador with an unusually long tail. This dog, said Andy, had a habit of wandering off and roaming about the country, sometimes for days, and anyone glimpsing it trotting through the trees, with its snub nose and feline tail, could easily imagine they were looking at a black puma.

It was disappointing when I subsequently presented Andy's theory to the six witnesses and they all more or less accepted it. 'Yes, I suppose it could have been a dog,' they said. But the air in the woods began to feel less tense, and when I eventually saw the animal myself I knew it was safe to go back into the dark. In fairly good light, on an October evening, it ran out of a clump of hawthorns and crossed the corner of a field. From fifty yards I could see it was a dog. It ran with a low, slinky heaviness and it had a very long tail.

It *was* a dog – wasn't it?

12

THE UNKNOWN

I do not possess a watch. If mechanical time runs too quickly for the slow procession of midsummer then it could never synchronize to the shifty rhythm of night. With its phases, pauses and unpredictable slips, night not only contradicts the clock, it makes a mockery of it. So it was impossible to say how long I had been in the trees. It felt like hours, but when I emerged again onto the open hill the moon had not curved much further westwards, nor had the glow beyond the northern skyline noticeably increased. The world, though, was like morning after the pitch-dark interior of the wood.

Everything seemed on a grander scale; the valley I'd walked through earlier now appeared deeper and the thin layer of mist along it had become a broad, white river; the line of trees to the west, which looked so close when the deer sneaked up behind me, had withdrawn to a vast distance, while the northern skyline loomed much higher than before. If distances had extended, close up detail was crystal clear. At my feet a half moon glistened in the dewdrops of individual grass blades, and where a late-blossoming elder leaned across the path I could make out each tiny five-pointed floret.

In the dark beneath the trees almost everything had been invisible, but the appeal of a midnight wood is in its sounds rather than sights – sounds like the manic chattering of a family of badgers, the echoing call of an owl or the toy-train chuffing of an amorous hedgehog. Yet despite my earlier predictions that the night would be rustling with life all I heard after the pigeon and the running fox was a skittering woodmouse and the curse of a crow that I disturbed on its nest. It seemed that most of the nightlife had already slipped into the moonlight where, if I kept my head down, I might meet it later. It was a relief, after the tangled wood, to be able to walk across open ground again, so with light steps but at a good pace I set off over the shoulder of the hill and down into the shadow of another valley, one that inclined east between trees before curving northward towards the higher slopes.

As is normal at night, the air was cooler on the valley floor, but less misty than along the previously travelled valley. Though the moon was not high enough to shine onto it, the grassy path was perfectly visible and, anyway, the deeper darkness more clearly revealed a point of greenish light, like a fallen star, fifty yards ahead. It was a glow worm and as I approached I could see it was clinging to a grass stem on the side of the path. Without disturbing it, I knelt down and placed a hand so that the strange light reflected on my palm.

A not uncommon gem in this area, the luminescent insect emerges from cover in the late evening and shines her hopeful beacon until dawn when she creeps back into her underground bed. Not quite an inch long, the female glow worm looks like a stretched woodlouse but is in fact a wingless beetle. The large-eyed winged males are half her size, possess a much feebler glow and are more beetle-ish in appearance. But I read recently that the female's seductive gleam has been failing to attract overflying males because the boys have been lured away by the brighter lights that now illuminate so much of the rural night. While this may be true, and just recently a male glow worm appeared in a lamplit room at home, it cannot help that vast tracts of the glow worm's natural habitat have been degraded by insecticide and herbicide spraying, over-grazing, and general disturbance. There are not many bright lights to confuse the males in this landscape, yet the female on the grass stem was only the third I have seen this season. A few years ago, on a similar June night, the path was lit up on both sides, like an elfen village street, by dozens of them.

I wished the insect a glowing future and continued up the valley, passing the remains of a long-dead ash tree that used to be home to a pair of barn owls, another species I see less of than in former times. A bird that was certainly not any kind of owl, nor any night-flying fowl that I know, uttered a weird *ka-kack, ka-kack-kack-kack* from the treeline on my left. It had to be a bird because the sound was travelling too quickly away from me for it to be anything else, though I suppose it could have been a banshee with a sore throat. Maybe tomorrow I will describe it to one of my more knowledgable bird-brained friends; and though he will probably laugh and say surely I realized it was an ordinary late-migrating something-or-other, my hope is that he will be as mystified as me. But writing about that bird call now has reminded me that last year, slightly later in the season, I was walking home under the stars with a friend when we heard the same sound. Having just passed a small copse we both spun round because the call had come from the trees and, by its sudden uplift, told us that it must be a bird that was now airborne. The copse was silhouetted by the evening's fading afterglow yet neither of us saw anything flying above it, although by the call's extraordinary loudness, the bird must have been quite large. After the sound had echoed to silence I looked at my friend, and her pale expression was a nice mix of wonder and shock.

The element of uncertainty is one of night's special pleasures. Sometimes it is more interesting *not* to know, and though I am familiar with most of the common nocturnal wildlife in this country I like the fact that, half seen or half heard, the identity of something is often open to interpretation. Especially in an age that craves accurate information, precise observation and instant recognition, I find a perverse delight in night's less definable reality. Though it offers a unique window onto my local wildlife, it also answers my desire for somewhere different, undisturbed and often unknown.

13

ACROSS THE DIVIDE

The lack of visual clutter in the nocturnal landscape makes even the most fleetingly glimpsed movement stand out like a bird shadow gliding across a bare wall, though the cause of the movement is often obscure. As I walked through a narrow, moonless stretch of valley something nudged the right-hand edge of my vision and when I looked round towards a line of anthills or maybe molehills up against the pale northern skyline I was intrigued to see that one of them was alive. By the time I'd remembered my binoculars it was almost out of sight. I was, apparently, looking along an animal's back, and though I refocused carefully it was impossible to tell whether the creature was heading away from or towards me so completely was it merging into the dark of the slope. Lowering the glasses, I took a few steps forward, altering my angle of perpective until the silhouette reappeared, definitely getting closer. Through the binoculars it looked like a potato sack bumping down the grassy decline. I had to kneel to keep it back-lit by the sky, yet even when it was less than thirty yards away and veering slightly to my right I still could not discern the striped head, though it was obvious by then that I was looking at a badger. The broad, humped shape and wallowing gait showed it to be a large male, possibly over thirty pounds in weight. I put my binoculars away as it slowed down and stopped at the foot of the slope. It raised its head, and for a moment I thought it had caught my scent.

Without the backdrop of sky to define it the badger, though only twenty paces away, was just a dark smudge in the grass, yet the familiar black and white mask now showed quite clearly. I remained still, with my hands in my pockets – hands that, in the night, show up as pale as a face. The animal stared fixedly at me, as if trying to decide what sort of thing I was. The brief impasse made me want to smile, but I have learnt that, though their eyesight is not the sharpest in the night, the slightest movement, even a change of facial expression, can spook a wary badger. Stillness is often as effective as concealment when observing wildlife so long as the stillness is *comfortably* absolute – relaxed rather than frozen.

Though I could see a badger almost any evening if I waited quietly on the downwind side of a sett, I rarely meet one face to face on open ground. Away from the security of its home a badger is liable to dash for cover if its fine senses register the slightest alarm; however, despite being inquisitive, my visitor was apparently unperturbed because he slowly ambled towards me, sniffing occasionally, until he had halved the distance between us. He raised his head once more and also seemed to stand on tiptoe so he could examine my shape at a slightly more equal level. We stared at one another across an ancient history that I could only imagine but to which he still belonged. Since the last Ice Age he had inherited this landscape and despite all the ensuing changes he was still perfectly adapted to it. I, however, represented the upright hunter-gatherer whose shadow had lengthened and darkened over thousands of years, and who had now become nothing but a clumping, dangerous interloper. Even if he sensed that I personally was no threat he still made me feel out of place for I was the only creature wandering about without clear pupose, the only thing that was not actively partaking in the task of survival. Like all wild animals, he could not afford to pause for long in his search for food, and though he no longer had any natural enemies his ancestral memory of human persecution would always keep him alert.

The meeting probably lasted about a minute, though that is a long time to be held in the gaze of a wild animal. And as the badger slowly turned and lumbered away I felt less alienated because his dismissive sniff was, I'm sure, a gesture of acceptance.

14

WATCHING
AND WAITING

When I was very young, before I had learnt how to fish or how to catch lizards, my knowledge of natural history might have been limited to whatever I could glean from my few illustrated nature books or the early television programmes of Peter Scott and David Attenborough, but my enthusiasm for the subject was boundless. However, were it not for one or two chance encounters with the local fauna, the whole idea of 'wildlife' might have remained in my childhood imagination as an ethereal community whose only trace lay in the curious pathways in the woods and the unidentified rustlings in the undergrowth. I could refer to my books if I wanted to get an idea of a particular animal's appearance, but it was only if I came across the real physical thing in its natural surroundings that I could believe in it.

Up to the age of ten or eleven, because I was afraid of the dark, the only wild mammals I happened upon, apart from my friends, were diurnal or semi-diurnal, like deer, hedgehogs, rabbits, hares and, very occasionally, stoats, weasels and, once, a suddenly surfacing mole. From my bedroom window I had heard foxes barking eerily at night and I sometimes glimpsed a russet blur dissolving into shadows, but it was not until the arctic winter of 1962/63 that I had my first clear, close-up view. During that extended freeze I would often see foxes hunting or scavenging in the snow in the middle of the day, and by the spring of '63 my district as well as many other semi-rural and suburban areas had been permanently settled by them. And now, of course, they have spread out into towns and cities. (Here, where much of the land is preserved mainly for partridge and pheasant, the fox remains as elusive as it was during my childhood.)

I liked the description and illustration of a badger in my *Children's Encyclopaedia*. After reading about their setts, their well-defined paths and their habits I guessed that if I wanted to see a real specimen I would have to embark on a deliberate quest rather than hope for a random meeting. Unfortunately, badgers were nocturnal, and though I could begin searching for one in the half-light I would probably have to brave the dark before anything appeared.

My first attempt was more a test of nerve than a proper hunt. I had discovered what I thought was a badger sett quite close to the edge of a local wood, close enough to an exit should the dark prove too menacing. After telling my mother I was just going out for a walk, I sauntered over to the wood on an evening in late summer. Settling down behind a tree within sight of the supposed sett, I began to wait and watch. It was exciting to begin with. I was on a proper voyage of discovery and could count it a huge success even if a badger only partially materialized because no one in my world had ever seen one before. But the leaves around me gradually lost their colour while, towards the interior, the tree trunks lost their texture and began merging together. Along the wood's edge the trees stood blackly against the still-glowing sky and the comfortingly yellow cornfield. It was only visibility that was changing; the stillness did not become more still as there was no dying breeze nor did the silence intensify as it was too late into the year for birdsong.

I had read that badgers often emerged at dusk and hoped this was true because what chance would I have of seeing one when the light was finally gone? As the shadows thickened there was the inevitable owl call, which signalled to the nether world that I was on my own in a wood that, though once familiar, would soon be transformed into a place I had always feared. The fact that nothing stirred by the sett only increased my anxiety for my attention remained fixed on the steadily deepening tide and the thought that, even if I was able to swim back to the edge of the trees I would probably still drown in the dark flooding the fields. Yet I had walked with friends across those fields on winter nights and felt nothing but delight at the sense of freedom the dark gave us. There was nothing to be fearful of – except that I knew that none of my pals would enter the woods at night, and now I was quietly sitting beneath those same trees I would surely discover the true ghastly reason why no sensible person should ever do such a thing. It seemed, therefore, that the badgers would be able to enjoy another few nights without me. I crept slowly out into the open, hoping nothing demonic would notice me, and ran home under the stars.

Maybe a month later I went back to the wood in daylight. How charmingly innocuous it seemed and how ordinary now that everything stood out so plain and unambiguously. A rabbit diving down one of the holes made me suspect that it had never been a proper sett in the first place. So, following the many narrow paths through the trees, I searched for a more badgerish-looking spot, yet the paths seemed only to lead to more rabbit burrows. Eventually I found a cavernous hole between the roots of a large oak tree, but there were no signs of recent activity and the dead leaves in the entrance looked as if they had been undisturbed for months. However, I liked the feel of the place and decided to keep watch on it until the light began to sink. It was too deep in the wood for me to stay much beyond sunset; apart from anything else, a person might easily become lost trying to find his way out in the dark – lost, or eaten.

Rather than hiding behind a tree and peering round, as I had done before, I made myself comfortable sitting on a mossy stump in full view of anything that might appear. I reasoned that if I kept still I could easily be mistaken for part of the stump. A breeze sprang up while I waited and the wood became noisy with the sound of rustling leaves, but it was only a passing gust that died away as the evening began to close in. The light was fading and yet for no obvious reason I suddenly felt less concerned, almost at ease with the idea of darkness. I ate an apple and tossed the core towards the hole, hoping it might tempt something into view. Ferns and fallen branches blurred together as the evening sank towards night, but the pale core, five yards away, showed up almost luminously. I kept my eyes fixed on it as the minutes passed, almost staring it into invisibility, and then I gave a little jump of astonishment as it actually vanished. There was not the slightest scrape or shiver of sound, and yet when it was almost too late I realized a badger had come in from one side, stolen the apple core and was somehow walking silently away as if floating on air. Its large, grey shape appeared transparent in the gloom, but when it reached the entrance of its sett it paused and half turned, revealing the clear profile of its striped muzzle.

15

THE GOOD SHEPHERD

As this landscape, which is like a great chalk island, rises towards its highest levels in the north-west it becomes ever more exquisitely folded into deep valleys, hollows and vales. Some of the tracks that run through these numerous depressions eventually lead, like paths in a maze, to a dead end, confronting the walker with a steep hundred-foot-high grassy or wooded incline. Even in daylight, getting lost can be easier than whistling unless you know the terrain or carry a map. At night, especially when the sky was clouded, the paths would often lead me in unexpected directions. During my first nocturnal forays here, twenty-five years ago,

I frequently lost my way, but it never concerned me much because, unlike getting lost on a cloud-capped mountain or in a big, trackless forest, the only danger was that I might get a little hungry and thirsty before I found my way home again.

Despite appearing quite dramatic from a low perspective this is, like all downland, easy country: easy to walk through, easy to climb, easy to get lost in, easy to get unlost in. After dark, if a path led me into a blind alley, I would simply climb the nearest slope and get my bearings from a familiar line of trees or hills. And however disoriented I sometimes became, if the sky was clear there were always the waymarking stars. It was good, though, to get lost now and then, if only because it always made the country seem larger and somehow more vivid. Moreover, being lost gave me an excuse, if I needed it, for wandering down paths I had no right to be on. Unfortunately I don't get lost much nowadays, though that does not mean the terrain has nothing new to offer. It can appear different with each new day, even by the hour as its contours turn under the sun or its hills blur into cloud. At night it is always offering new insights into its natural history, just as it sometimes seems to be remembering its almost equally ancient human history, which goes back further than Anglo-Saxon and Roman encampments and beyond the burial mounds of the Iron Age.

A ghost hunter would probably find this landscape trembling with haunted sites, and though I don't believe in ghosts any more I like the way a place can become 'ghostly' simply because a change in conditions charges its atmosphere with a new energy. As an inveterate night fisher and night walker I have experienced several richly spooky moments that, had I not been accustomed to night's weirdnessess, might have converted me to the ghost-hunter's cause.

The best approximation of a ghost I ever saw drifted across a clearing in a Surrey yew wood one autumn night many years ago. It had the classic look, a seven-foot-tall luminous shroud, and it managed an almost complete circuit of the small glade before spinning itself into a vaporous funnel and dissolving into air. Though it is not uncommon to see fingers of vapour emerging from a wood's warm interior during a cold night, this one had somehow formed itself into a perfect and surprisingly long-lasting phantom. I really should have asked it its name. The finest ghost to materialize amongst these hills was also born out of mist. On a cool night in late summer I was walking along one of the deeper valleys when, thirty yards ahead, a white fallow deer stepped out of a bank of white fog. For a few spectral moments we stood facing one another before the deer slowly climbed the left-hand slope and faded into the trees. Had I not seen the same animal twice before on less atmospheric nights I might have thought it more miraculous, but it was still a lovely apparition.

It is ten years now since I saw the white fallow, but when, last night, I came to the place where we previously met I thought I might see other ordinary members of its herd. The lush grass of the slopes makes it a favourite spot for both fallow and roe deer, and I have often seen their silhouettes parading elegantly along the skyline above me. But last night, though I stood and watched for a while, nothing showed – at least not just there.

As I waited, I noticed that the northern sky had grown a shade paler along its eastern half. There were still a few bright stars, including one that must have been a planet – Jupiter or maybe Saturn; and, all the while, the bit of Earth I was standing on was more obviously tilting towards dawn. Had I been on top of the nearby hill I might have heard a far-off church clock strike three.

Thinking about the temporary absence of fallow deer and the ubiquitous presence of ghosts that were not ghosts, I turned up a track that climbed steeply towards the northern ridge. Everything suddenly became lighter as the moon reappeared over the lower slopes behind me. Where the track levelled out there stood a large, solitary ash tree with widely outspreading branches. Gathered beneath, in dappled moonlight, was a small flock of sheep, all lying on the grass. Though they kept their eyes on me not one stirred, for the tree was their protector and, anyway, they sensed my harmlessness. It was a timeless scene, like a painting by Samuel Palmer, or maybe a parable from the Old Testament: the good shepherd standing over his flock. But in response to my vision one of them farted magnificently, and so I continued on my way.

16

THE BLUE-EYED BIRD

Although certain corners of this landscape may remain silent throughout a June night, as I walk through the varied terrain there will, if I pause to listen, usually be some audible signs of life, even if it is only the scurrying of a vole or the scream of an imperilled rabbit; and whenever I pass a stretch of woodland there is nearly always the familiar wheezing of owlets as they plead with their parents for more mice. Ten miles eastward, however, where the geology changes from chalk to greensand, the different habitat of pine forest and heath echoes with a very different sound.

I was talking about this sound recently because, when he stepped into my house for a cup of tea and a chat, a friend's first word was 'nightjar'. Colin had spotted the gnarled piece of wood that sits up behind the light fitting on the living-room wall. It had been saved from the stove last winter as I thought its bird shape resembled a nightjar, and I was pleased my visitor agreed as he knows more about these birds than I do. The species does not inhabit my local woods and, while I poured the tea, I told Colin that I had not heard their distinctive call since I used to fish a lake in a forest to the east many years ago. Colin knew that stretch of country intimately, owned as it is by the Forestry Commission who employ him as a deer ranger. From May to July, whenever his work extended into the late evenings, he said he often heard the nightjar's churr. I told him I would like to reacquaint myself with that sound and in exchange for a second pot of tea Colin invited me to his favourite part of the forest. Perhaps unwisely, he said he could almost guarantee the birds would sing for me.

A week later, early in the evening, Colin arrived again at my house and we headed eastward in his pick-up across the county border. As we drove the dozen or so miles we discussed the other types of creature we might see or hear. Being aware of my enthusiasm for reptiles, Colin said that because the day had been warm there was an outside chance of spotting the only species of British snake I had never seen: the smooth snake. There were also sand lizards and adders, all of which offered us something striking to look out for before the sun went down and the nightjars became active.

Although walkers, horse riders and cyclists are free to follow the woodland tracks, only foresters and the deer ranger are permitted to drive along them, which was probably just as well as Colin's territory was spread across several square miles and he did not want to be out all night. Having unlocked a gate we chugged slowly through a belt of trees, emerging onto a patch of open ground where Colin suddenly braked because a fallow buck was watching us from a nearby slope. In all the years he had spent stalking deer this was the first fallow he'd ever seen in the forest.

'Maybe it's a good omen,' I said, and we trundled on.

We followed a steep sandy track to the top of a high ridge where we could look around and I could get a proper sense of the treescape. The evening air was dense with the resinous scent of pine, so different from the herb-salad air of chalk downland. Below us, dark rows of spire-tipped trees stretched away into the distance, and as we scanned them Colin spotted another deer, the type he usually expects to see: the roe deer. Yet though he pointed out its position in the trees and told me the direction it was heading I did not see it until it materialized in a clearing about a hundred and fifty yards away. I thought my eyesight was quite good, but even with binoculars I had not seen the animal amongst the branches. However, Colin remarked that after thirty years of deer stalking he recognized how the changing patterns in light and shadow indicated an animal's presence, however dense the undergrowth; moreover, he was sure it was the same for me, being able to detect a fish moving beneath the surface that would be invisible to an untrained eye.

We climbed back into the vehicle and zig-zagged along miles of sometimes boggy, sometimes dusty paths until we came to a south-facing slope of heather and bracken with just a few isolated stands of Scots pine. Though his main task in the forest is deer management, Colin is also the steward and protector of everything from dunnock to dormouse, sparrowhawk to stagbeetle, and these responsibilities include the improvement of habitat. A few years ago, in an effort to encourage the local reptile life, he cleared pine and birch saplings from a few acres of hillside, knowing the increased sunlight would improve the ground cover. Once the heather was more established Colin laid some yard-square sheets of corrugated iron randomly across it and within a few weeks several adders and smooth snakes had moved into their new homes. (For years I have had a similar reptile shed on my patch of 'lawn' and though it has never attracted any snakes the native slow worms treat it as a luxury hotel.) Colin's rusted bits of metal were still in place and we began searching for them through knee-deep undergrowth. Because the sun had by then almost set and the air was cooling rapidly I was told not to raise my hopes. With now cold metal above them, Colin surmised that any snakes would probably have slid away into the heather roots.

There were a dozen covers to inspect but we hunted over a wide area before we eventually located one and gently lifted it up – to reveal Britain's rarest reptile. Colin was as amazed as me, not just because we had discovered one at our first attempt, but that we had found one at all. For a second we remained absolutely still. The tightly coiled serpent did not panic or hiss; it simply raised its head a fraction and calmly regarded us with its dark eyes. It was a beautiful-looking animal, steel grey, darkly spotted along its back, with a vivid black stripe along the side of its small head. Its scales were so perfectly interlocked that I wanted to pick it up to discover just how smooth it really felt, yet I resisted the temptation. Though the dip in temperature had made it docile I didn't want to disturb it, and after a long minute we lowered its roof and left it in peace.

I said that a single smooth snake had made my summer. It was also the first Colin had seen this year, but in the interest of science he wanted to check the other snake sheds. We eventually located all twelve without finding so much as a snail under any of them.

The light was fading by the time we were travelling again, this time along a straight track towards a rising line of fir trees. During the snake hunt there had been a chorus of birdsong, including calls from species I never hear at home, like the tree pipit and the wood-lark, but as the evening deepened the day songs were not replaced by night songs. As we entered a denser tract of forest our road turned sharply around the edge of a wide clearing and we stopped where a large pine leaned over us. After the engine was switched off I thought the fan must have remained whirring until I realized I was listening to a nightjar. We climbed out of the cab and though the bird fell silent it appeared out of the treetop overhead, circling us at about thirty feet and slapping its pointed wings in what I presumed was a display of aggression. But then it uttered what I knew was the mating call – a piercing *chi-koo, chi-koo* – and, as we watched, a female darted out of the trees to join it. They looked like miniature hawks; and though only visible for a few moments in semi-darkness they were so close that we could clearly see their speckled plumage and the male's bold white flashes. I suspected Colin had known they were nesting somewhere nearby, but he just laughed, saying that while he'd hoped we might hear one he'd not expected to be buzzed by one.

As the first stars appeared so other nightjars began to make their voices heard, some close by, others far off, their eerie wavering monotone gradually building into layers of sound more akin to a field of crickets than a forest of birds – or, maybe, more like a factory of sewing machines, then I can say that I was listening to an *industry* of nightjars.

We drove on again, trundling a mile or so into a partially wooded valley where a thin mist suggested the presence of water. It was woodcock country, said Colin, as we stepped out again into the cool night air – air that was sweet with the scent of bog myrtle. Right on cue, as if once again the whole show had been arranged for my benefit, or I was taking part in a very predictable wildlife film, we immediately heard a woodcock's sharp call. Looking towards the sound, we spotted the bird flying slowly against the lingering twilight, roding along the edge of the trees. It called again, a high-pitched double whistle followed by a rather comic frog-like croak, then the repeated whistle. Like the nightjar's call, it is a sound I have never heard around my present home, but it winged me back to a time before parent-hood or marriage, when I lived with my wife-to-be in a cottage in the middle of a well-watered oak wood. On late evenings in spring and summer a woodcock would often call out as it flapped past our open window and I would sometimes hear it even in sleep.

Setting off once more, Colin said he had to be wary driving through the forest at night because, just occasionally, his headlights would pick out a nightjar sitting in the middle of the track, apparently dust bathing. He described how the bird's reflective eyes glowed bright blue if he shone the spotlight at them. The rotatable lamp was positioned on the cab's roof, operated from inside, and to demonstrate the power of its beam Colin switched it on to reveal, well beyond the range of the headlights, a pair of sparkling blue eyes. Our jaws dropped in astonishment. Colin braked, the nightjar remained sitting about a hundred yards ahead and, after a moment's hesitation, I focused my binoculars on it. In the glare of the spotlight it looked extraordinary, the eyes so supernaturally large and dazzling they obscured the outline of the bird itself. It did not seem bothered by the beam, yet when Colin switched it off and edged forward it darted away. A mile later another nightjar flickered in front of us, yet there were no others sitting on the tracks and Colin had only seen one other blue-eyed bird this year.

Were these events purely serendipitous, I wondered; were they proof of Colin's finely tuned hunter's instinct or perhaps the work of a benign forest god? But as we chugged along, instead of talking about the apparent magic of perfect timing we discussed the dangers faced by ground-nesting birds like nightjars and woodcocks. I asked Colin about the number of foxes, but he could not recall when he last saw one, nor was there much evidence of them. It was the same at home, I said – of all the local fauna the fox was the least visible, though I described how a tiny cub once wandered into the garden when I was having tea with my children. Refusing cake, it simply curled up in the long grass and went to sleep. Just as I was about to relate the story's happy ending, Colin said nervously, 'What's that?'

Bobbing along the track ahead of us was, of course, a very small fox cub. It dashed off into the trees as we carefully overtook it, yet we agreed it had not been a hallucination.

Everything we'd seen and heard had been real; it was only the circumstances that were fantastical. But, inspired by our run of luck, I predicted that simply by envisaging an encounter with two dream-like women we would surely meet them, lost in the forest, and we could politely offer them a lift home, probably to their fairy castle. We had not seen another human being all evening, but five minutes later my throat went dry as the headlights illuminated the wondrous prophesy. However, as we approached, we saw that it wasn't exactly as I had foretold. There were, as Colin will testify, two tall blondes walking through the dark, and though they looked lovely as we drew level with them, we also realized that something was walking along just ahead of them. We didn't, therefore, offer them a lift because there was not enough room in the back for their horse.

17

EDGES OF LIGHT

Looking north from the edge of these hills half the midsummer night is a false dawn. In midwinter, when the sky is clear, the dawn is only a brief blossoming of gaslight blue before the sun comes up, but in June it seems to begin as soon as the evening twilight tapers to a fingertip along the northern horizon. Last night I didn't notice that phase of lowest light as I was deep under the trees at the time; also the moon was vying for attention then, its glow in the south outshining yet never completely obscuring the shimmer in the north. However, by about three o'clock, as I climbed the northward path, everything that lay ahead of me —

trees, fenceposts, hedges, hilltops – was more clearly defined against the up-glow, though there were still two hours before sunrise.

The path was a long one, longer than it would have been had I forked left on a ridge and headed directly towards the nearest high point. But, on a whim, I suddenly decided to veer sharp right, following the ridge south-eastwards for a mile before turning north again round the edge of a wood. Ambling over the rabbit-cropped grass it was easy to slip into the slightly trancelike state that can happen to anyone during a solitary all-night walk, especially when the body is beginning to complain about lack of sleep. Because of the direction I was heading there was darkness above, a moonlit sky low to my right and the quarter-light of dawn to my left – parallel bands of brightness that, in my mind, became like a shining sea on one hand and the glow from a distant city on the other. Though I don't recall swinging left towards the wood, the auto-pilot was obviously set correctly because I gradually became conscious of foliage eclipsing the few remaining stars.

I was not, of course, wholly unaware of my surroundings, but the lack of activity over the previous hour had dulled my senses, and the smooth, familiar path had allowed me to almost walk myself asleep, until the sound of a wingbeat, soft but very close, jolted me to a big-eyed stop. Broad black wings spread out only a few yards above my head as a gigantic owl launched itself from an overhanging bough. For a moment I really did think it was an eagle owl – after all, it's not unknown for this species to occasionally drift over from the continent. But it was simply a trick of the dark. Before the bird blurred into the stars its clear outline told me that I had just disturbed a roosting and perfectly ordinary buzzard. Perhaps the silhouette had seemed more owlish because it was a downy, just-fledged youngster; then again it might have been an early-rising adult, not roosting at all, but scanning the dawn's edges for unsuspecting rabbits. And, if nothing else, it woke me to the realization that the atmosphere had changed.

As I stared into birdless space I could feel that the slow night-long current of cool northern air had been replaced by the vaguest feather of a breeze from the south. Nothing stirred, yet it seemed as if a flag had unfurled, signalling the official end of night.

Continuing along the eaves of the wood, I passed under a large ash that sounded as if it were humming to itself. Or was the sound only in my head? Stopping once more, I cupped my hands behind my ears, increasing the volume so that I could hear that the tree was alive with the faint high-pitched whine of a thousand insects. It was a sound I usually associate with hot summer afternoons in an oak wood when wasps and hoverflies buzz around honeydewed leaves, except this was of a higher frequency. Though it was too dark to see them, a hatch of small flies was celebrating the moist crepuscular hour when new life so often begins.

After another hundred yards, the path turned into the thicker dark of the wood, stretching like a tunnel towards the glow of a narrow opening on the far side. Halfway towards that exit I was stopped in my tracks yet again, this time because I heard the soft tread of a deer picking its way through the undergrowth. It drew invisibly closer, finally stepping out into the path in front of me, a formless black shape framed by the arch of blueish light beyond. It was a fallow buck and it stood absolutely still, its body profiled but its antlered head turned towards me. I was standing against a darker background, yet the deer could obviously see me in the pale glimmer, though it seemed inquisitive rather than fearful; like the badger earlier, it stared as if trying to decide whether or not I posed a threat. After a while it looked back along the way it had come and a moment later another deer appeared, a fallow doe that silently crossed the path and immediately melted into the darkness on the other side. The buck remained where he was, turning to stare at me again with invisible eyes. We stood twenty yards apart and I was just wondering how long we might spend in each other's company when an unexpected birdsong distracted me. Without moving my head I turned my eyes towards the sound, and when I looked back there was only an empty, dim-lit path.

18

THE EARLIEST BIRD

What bird was singing in the still-solid dark of the wood? Its distance and the density of the trees gave its voice a strange hollowness that blurred any recognizable phrasing and made it hard to identify. For a moment I wondered if it was a nightingale, even though it was over twenty years since I'd last heard one there, and then never so late in June. Though indistinct, I was certain it was not a thrush, yet the sound seemed too bell-like to be a blackbird and I couldn't think of another bird that had a similar-shaped sound. But then a second song began to rise up much closer to me, like a crystal-clear echo of the first, and it was a blackbird after all.

Within a few minutes there were four, all singing from different directions, and of course they were not perched under the canopy, where the light had yet to penetrate, but up in the treetops where the dawn was already brightening. I had been standing at the place where the deer had vanished and I could have happily remained there for another half-hour, listening to the other birds – mistle thrush, blackcap, robin and wren – as, one by one, they added their songs to the choir.

Unlike the chorus that wakes me in my bed almost every morning now, but only when it attains alarm-clock intensity, the one I hear at the end of a nightwalk builds gradually from a single voice; and even a corn bunting in an empty field can sound miraculous after the hours of silence. There is a sense of joy in it, as in the song at the end of winter, yet also fragility in its newness, as if it were the first bird that had ever sung. And, whatever the species, its own particular sound remains clear in my head, though the rest of the night will, over the years, eventually blur into other nights and other dawns.

Last year, the opening notes were sung by a swallow – the bird circling invisibly in the twilight – but usually they are uttered by a thrush, a robin or a woodpigeon. During the 1990s, for three years in succession, the earliest bird was a cuckoo (this year I have not heard one at all in this part of the country), while almost half a century ago my very first all-night walk ended beneath the high-altitude song of a skylark.

I used to be able to hear skylarks singing above the fields round my house but, like the nightingales, they are just a local memory now; however, up on the more remote and less sheep-grazed slopes there are still a few survivors; and when I eventually stepped out into the light at the end of the path I heard the once famil-iar liquid music falling from a distant point in the sky.

Walking towards the well-defined, dome-like radi-ance of the dawn, which seemed almost brilliant after the dark of the wood, there were still a few vague stars above me, though when I looked back the moon had lost its silver sheen. It must have been a little after four o'clock; still almost an hour – the most sublime hour of the day – before sunrise, and I didn't feel tired at all. Since the buzzard had startled me out of my semi-sleepwalk each little event had only served to sharpen the senses and increase my appreciation of the moment. By the time I heard the skylark I was not trudging slowly along like any sixty-three-year-old who had been up all night, but striding lightly like a ten-year-old starting his summer holidays. Yet it was not all joy. The dew on the tall grass was so heavy I was wading rather than walking. My new boots had proved comfort-able – the walk would have petered out by midnight had they pinched – but I'd ignored the bootmaker's weather-proofing advice. Moisture was beginning to seep through and my socks were as sad as old dishcloths. However, such clamminess was instantly forgotten when I spotted an owl flying low over the wheat field on my left. Initially it was no more than a distant silhouette coming straight towards me out of a dark blue sky. Could it, I wondered, be a barn owl, a bird I had not seen in that area for years? As it approached to within thirty yards it banked sharply so that its under-sides caught the light and revealed the lovely pearl white plumage. It fluttered round in a half-circle, becoming a silhouette again as it winged over the curve of the field.

19

THE HUNT

I leaned against a fencepost for a few minutes, hoping that the barn owl would reappear. It didn't, but while I watched the last star fading into the blue a pale moth floated past and landed amongst the tall grasses next to me. I think it was a white ermine, a lovely insect that I sometimes see flitting against lamp-lit windows at home, yet when I bent down to look I couldn't find it. Had I never seen one before I would have crawled carefully about on the dewy ground to investigate, just as I used to do when my knees were always wet or muddy and everything was unknown.

As a small child I was fairly awe-struck by each newly discovered creature, no matter what species, my reaction to, say, a centipede, being probably the same as an astronaut's if he or she had found one on Mars. As much as their first-timeness, what made these findings so startling was the realization that I was sharing a world with such marvels as ants, frogs, sticklebacks and dragonflies.

And when, thirty years later, I became a father I could watch my own litter enjoying the same enthusiasms and revelations, their behaviour reminding me that, like all children, they possessed a form of superior intelligence based not on study or personal experience but instant sensory appraisal. Whenever they found some new earthly being, they may have been ignorant of its name and classification yet they saw it in a perfect light. They recognized the grace of a slug as it glided between grass blades, they appreciated the industry as well as the murderous efficiency of a spider, they gasped at the delicacy of a gnat and they laughed at the freedom of a bird.

Mulling now over the events of last night, I'm thinking that one of the reasons an animal has more presence in the dark is simply because its glimpsed, half-seen shape tantalizes like the whole of nature did when I was an infant; despite being colourless and two dimensional it has the intensity that my innocent eye used to see everywhere. The sight of a hare outrunning its shadow across a sunlit field could never be less than captivating, but skylined by a field of stars it seems to loom right out of a dream, or a childhood vision.

Fined down by the dark to a symbol of itself, the image of a wild creature might also stir a more distant genetic memory from the time when it was painted on the wall of a cave. (I appreciate that my fondness for nocturnal apparitions does sometimes make me forget that the curious silhouette on a hill is in fact a living, breathing animal, but I like the suspicion of unreality.)

When I go fishing I always have one particular species in mind and, though I may not catch anything, the image of that fish, be it perch, tench or carp, will stay with me all day. Nightwalking is different because I rarely have such fixed intentions, the walk itself being a fairly random exercise and the observation of wildlife no more than a chance event. Yet even on a cloudy, moonless night with nothing much to see there is always the hope that something will show eventually. The hope, the expectation, gives a sense of purpose and after a mile or two a vision begins to form in my head, like the imaginary fish, but more obscure, more primal. My senses sharpen, my footfalls soften, and I have to stop and decode the slightest sound or movement. And so every walk becomes a hunt, just as every childhood run into the open air was a hunt.

I suppose I might not be so enthusiastic about nocturnal rambling if no wildlife ever appeared on my path, yet, however elusive the fauna, there will always be the stars to admire – heaven's eternal bonfires – and the moon in its various stages, and spectral mists and cloud formations unlike any that drift under the sun. Sometimes, just for the drama of it, I will bundle out into the heaviest storms, when there is nothing other than the roar of wind, the pounding of thunder and the scything of rain. I might not make more than a couple of miles in such conditions, but it is always exhilarating being bashed about by monstrous weather, especially as most of my nightwalking happens in stillness.

When I tell my diurnal friends about these things – not so much about the storms, but about the fact that the most ordinary stretch of countryside can be transformed by starlight into an area of outstanding natural beauty – they are not often convinced. They say that no one goes out after dark without a torch, or that dark can seem dire and, anyway, if a person wants to see the moon they can look from their bedroom windows. If I then go on to describe in loving detail the local nocturnal wildlife they will often just smile sympathetically, like my dry friends do whenever I enthuse too much about fishing.

'And why,' someone once asked me suspiciously, 'do you nearly always go out alone?'

Because, firstly, especially when the night is calm, one nightwalker is half as intrusive as two; and, secondly, I want the freedom to be able to wander or backtrack or deviate or pause or ruminate or even sleep, and only when I'm solitary do I have the luxury of such waywardness. On a bright, breezy day it's always a delight to walk over hills with friends or family, but at night I prefer to be on my own. There is more time if you don't have to share it, more time to concentrate on the things around you, as any child or hunter would understand.

20

Two Ways of Looking at a Sunrise

As it led up the last slope before the upper ridge my path skirted a deep combe overflowing with fine mist. The cool saturated air that had been collecting all night at the lower levels was being herded along by the southern shift until it had nowhere else to go except up and over the hollow's northern rim. A thin plume drifted diagonally and very slowly across the path, slightly blurring the way ahead, and as I walked through it I could feel its moisture like a refreshing balm on my face. It tasted of watercress.

The birdsong faded as I drew further from the wood, but I gradually became aware of a new sound as a long line of stunted beeches up on the ridge caught the beginnings of a breeze. Just a few yards down the slope, though the mist crept forward, there was not a tremble of any grass blade or wheat stem, yet the skylined trees were visibly swaying, making a whisper like a far-off ocean. Only when I was next to them could I feel the air moving. A steady and surprisingly warm draught was coming in from the south, smelling of gardens after rain.

The trees were planted early last century as a protective windbreak for the fields that sloped down on either side, hundreds of acres of once pristine down-land given over to the production of cereals. Fortunately, in this high area of the chalk, because of the steeper scarps and narrow vales, there are almost as many acres where the plough could never furrow, so there is enough wild grass for deer as well as sheep, enough space for hare as well as pheasant and partridge, though not perhaps enough wild flowers for all the insects nor enough areas of unkempt scrub for the songbirds.

I looked back across the still-shadowy landscape and tried to trace the zig-zagging route I'd taken through the night. There were certain landmarks – groupings of trees, a lovely upward curve of a hill – that were easy to recognize; others, however, seemed puzzling, though I could not ponder them for long as time was pressing. Time had not truly existed for me once the first stars had appeared last evening. Several eternities seemed to have passed since then, but now I had to realign myself with the idea of the clock or risk missing a possible grand finale. Pushing through the avenue, I emerged on the high north-facing edge of the downs with my ultimate objective almost in sight. Over to my right was a grassy promontory that jutted out like the prow of a ship into the level fields far below. With the north-eastern skyline beginning to blossom with colour, I needed to hurry across to the headland's far side. The time, I reckoned, was around quarter to five, the official sunrise moment at Greenwich for this day. However, being well over a hundred miles west of Greenwich, there would be several minutes delay for me to find my spot and prepare for the upblaze.

As a once habitual night fisher I must have seen a thousand summer sunrises (together with their reflections), yet I still find them compelling and powerful whichever way I look at them, and, as long as the glare is not too intense, there are always two ways of looking at a sunrise. Furthermore, every dawn is different; one morning the sun looks like a ghost peach as it rises through bands of mist, the next it comes up furnace white as the barometer starts to fall. Sometimes the variations are more subtle, almost unnoticable, yet the mood of the day is often determined by them.

I marched quickly across the shoulder of the hill and hopped over a fence that ran along the edge of a steep north-east-facing slope. This, I decided, was my destination. Taking off my jacket, I spread it on the wet grass, sat down and leant back against a fencepost. The horizon's rosy blush was still quite subdued, which meant there was plenty of time before the finale to catch my breath and contemplate a landscape flooding with light. Below me was a four-hundred-foot-deep U-shaped vale. There was no mist at the foot of the slope, but, further off, pale layers hung horizontally across the vale's entrance, extending towards and around a line of low, treeless hills in the middle distance. Beyond those hills was another ridge, bristling with pinewoods, and then another and another – seven rows of hills in all, each one floating, seemingly weight-less, in different densities of mist.

The breeze that had been stirring the beeches on the high ridge behind me was unnoticable on the leeward side and the rustling of leaves was almost inaudible from my position. There were a few far-off bird calls, but the open slopes around me were mostly silent. On the incline below and to my left a small herd of cows was standing motionless, each animal looking out from the hill as if, like me, waiting for something to happen.

Along the skyline a ribbon of transparent cloud began to smoulder, turning from amber to gold in the moments before the sun finger-tipped into view. First there was a thin, almost purplish sliver, then a not quite dazzling half-disc, easy to follow as it heaved itself slowly, minute by minute, into full view. But by concentrating while also remembering some elemen-tary astronomy I told myself, as I always like to do at both sunrise and sunset, that I was gazing at an illu-sion. And as the skyline sank *down* over the sun's face so I briefly observed the actuality and immensity of Earth's perpetual spin. At daybreak the sun does not, of course, rise; the Earth sinks, and whenever I am properly conscious of this I think I also feel the horizon's forward motion, which, in turn, somehow makes the entire landscape seem less remote and more intimate. However, I can never maintain this perspective for long.

As soon as a gap opened between the skyline and the sun I lost all sense of the planet pitching like a ship and reverted once more to the original idea of the sun climbing into the heavens and us at the still centre.

21

THE HIGHEST SONG
IN THE SKY

Having raised my green plastic water bottle to the just-risen sun I downed the contents in one long, refreshing swirl. I had rationed myself to only a few sips through the night because I knew that, by dawn, water with a sprig of apple mint would taste delicious. To follow there was oat flapjack, but as I prepared to munch into it a skylark rose up directly in front of me.

Since I sat down on the hill, about fifteen minutes earlier, there had been songs from whitethroat and greenfinch, but nothing else close by and not even a distant skylark. Yet here was one that must have been sitting just a few paces down the slope from me and so perfectly aligned that he flicked past the sun as he spired vertically upwards. His fluid song began as soon as he took to the air and it continued unbroken as he rose higher – and higher. I grabbed my binoculars before he faded from sight, focusing on him just as he executed a neat swivel. The first half of his ascent had been through almost still air, facing the sun, but then he must have felt the high southerly breeze behind him and so, without missing a wingbeat, turned against it to gain height more easily.

Even through the lenses the bird was soon no more than a slightly trembling dot in the sky. He began to hover and so, keeping his position in sight, I slowly put the binoculars to one side; but it took me a patient minute before I eventually picked him out again with the naked eye. Had I only been aware of him by his song I could never have found him unaided, yet, despite his height from the ground the song remained surprisingly clear and bright. This hill, he declared, and this sky is *my* domain.

It can be difficult to judge the altitude of a small high-flying bird, even if it's hovering, but the lark was, I thought, unusually high, maybe five hundred feet above the hilltop. As the hill is itself eight hundred feet above sea level the song could have been the highest in southern England. Yet despite its solitary beauty it was a pity that it was not just one voice in a great skylark choir of the kind that used to halleluia over those hills just a generation ago.

Maybe it was the lingering effect of the minted water, but as I lay on my back, listening upwards, I began to think about different birdsong in terms of taste, as some people – synaesthetes – hear sound in terms of colour. I decided that the skylark's song was like the taste of apricot while the thrush's was closer to the tartness of freshly picked gooseberry. A bullfinch's soft call is the taste of pear and the song of a wren has the intensity of a clementine, but the blackbird's voice has both the delicacy of a blueberry plus the velvet depth of vintage grape.

As I relaxed my focus, not because of lack of sleep but because the skylark's undulatory song was so mesmeric, the speck of him merged into the sky and disappeared, and maybe two or three minutes later he fell abruptly silent. I stared up again more intently and in a while he reappeared, rapidly descending on parachute wings, coming straight back down to his starting point where maybe his mate waited with their nestlings in the tussocky grass.

22

MONDAY MORNING

The sun had risen, but the world below me did not become more solid; in fact it looked less substantial than it was in the dark – more afloat in illuminated air than rooted. And though clear of mist, even the slopes around me shimmered with a curious light. I had not been aware of them earlier, but the sunlight revealed a hillside festooned with thousands of small, neat spider-webs. They were stretched horizontally between grass blades, all exactly the same size, no larger than the span of my hand. Every inch of silk was hung with dewdrops so that, when I looked closely, it appeared that each web was delicately woven from strings of tiny sun-reflecting pearls. The accumulated light was almost wintry, as if the grass were covered with frost.

I remembered my flapjack and contentedly ate it, but, wanting something more, was disappointed to find that as I was sitting on my jacket I had somehow squashed a banana and milled a packet of crisps that had been in one of the pockets. The two items could have been mixed into a gluey, salty muesli, though fortunately just the idea was enough to cure my hunger.

By the sun it was a little past five o'clock. A Monday morning, a sublime morning, yet to the birds on the hill it was not much different to any other when the summer sky is clear. Though their songs sounded like a hymn to the sunrise, they were only sound-marking their territory or appealing for a mate, and they will sing just as beautifully tomorrow, even if it's raining. Apart from their mostly far-off voices and the faint rustling of leaves up on the ridge there were no other sounds. Not even the hyper-sensitive ears of a bat or owl could have heard the industry that was going on amongst the spiders in the grass and there was, as yet, nothing else happening. Had the airflow been from the north instead of the south I might have heard a drone from a miles-distant road, or the rumble from an even more distant railway, not that there was probably much moving in that other world just then. It was too early even for a farmer on a tractor and now that the sheep had lambed there would be no quad-biking shepherds for hours. I could, therefore, continue to savour the dawn uninterrupted, my senses not yet dulled through tiredness, in fact still quite sharp and interestingly focused after a night of creaturely encounters.

One of the joys of walking a long night path is the way in which everything in my head gradually clears of mundane domestic concerns and personal anxieties, as if I were walking-off a slight headache or a hangover. And because no one can reach me or knows where I am (I could never own a mobile phone), because I know that apart from the animals I will always, unless I meet a deer poacher, be in perfect solitude, I am therefore able to bring all my attention to bear on the present moment. Normally, the present is just a transition point, a bit of a blur between one thing and the next, yet in the untroubled and mostly unrevealing dark, past and future have less relevance and I can find

myself in a place of endless immediacy, a place known
to every wild animal, a timelessness.

In that other Monday morning all the clocks were
getting ready to take over. Throughout the night they
had been swinging their hands in futile gestures, but
soon they would be in command again. However, on
the hill, I was once more the focus of an animal's
unblinking gaze. A female roe deer had inched her
head above the downward curve of the slope, maybe a
hundred yards below me. At first she was just a pair of
ears that I initially thought were dock leaves that must
have moved in a breeze. But then her head and long
neck slowly appeared and, equally slowly, I raised my
binoculars to admire her lovely big-eyed face. She
must have caught my scent, and, made curious, wanted
to investigate; but though, as mentioned earlier, this
often occurs with inquisitive bucks I had never before
experienced such behaviour in a doe.

Backlit by the low sun, her image through the
lenses had almost the same enigmatic quality as a
nocturnal silhouette, though now I was able to study
her in detail. As she gradually approached I could see
that her eyes were not, as I first thought, staring fixedly

at me. Her head remained pointing forward, but the eyes constantly swivelled from side to side, her expression reminding me of someone who cannot quite believe what they're doing. Her nostrils never stopped twitching. This was not a pampered park deer; it was a wild animal, perfectly aware of the dangers of humans. Under normal daylight conditions I'm convinced she would have fled as soon as she spotted me.

How close, I wondered, would she come? It was comical, the way she was trying to be invisible by moving like a snail, and for at least five minutes I watched her hesitant slow-motion advance until she went out of focus and I had to lower the glasses. She was right next to me, which made me laugh in surprise, and of course that was too much for her and she leapt back down the hill.

I should have stayed silent and still; perhaps she just wanted to whisper something in my ear.

23

THE SONOROUS
RAVEN

Only when the sun had climbed well above the skyline
did I really begin to feel its heat, the warmth on my face
tempting me to tilt my hat down, lie back and glide
away into a necessary oblivion. It seemed an age since
I was similarly tempted while watching the cold moon,
but even though I was now carrying more weight of
miles, even though everything was beginning to weave
a sleepiness around me – the sky was a deep-sleep blue
and the birds sang sleep-sweet songs – I resisted the
desire. After all, I thought, I should not be *that* tired.

The advantage of an all-night walk that begins on a
Sunday is that, on that day, none of my family ever stirs

until the afternoon. Therefore I, too, am guaranteed an epic slumber, maybe twelve hours of it, which is important if I am going to walk all the way to Monday. Also, though it would have been delightful to dream on that hilltop, I think I would have felt almost guilty about shutting my eyes on such a radiant morning, even for just a few minutes; there was no telling what I might have missed.

A cup of tea would have helped, though. In previous years I have occasionally driven out along one of the lanes before the walk and secreted a complete tea-making kit in a tree somewhere near the end of the planned walk. Yet however memorable the resultant brew when I returned to the tree again next dawn, I resist such careful preparation nowadays: not only does it require too much time and effort, it also requires me to head towards a predetermined spot. Especially at night, I prefer the freedom to meander in unpredictable directions.

This time I could not even be bothered to make myself a sandwich, but then it is the walk that matters, not the victuals. However long the path, an apple, something from the biscuit tin and a bottle of water will usually suffice until I get home. I could never carry the tea kit on the walk itself as to go on a night stroll is to go quietly and soft-footed – I want to feel as light as paper when I'm walking up the slopes, not weighed down with sloshing, clinking tea things. (I used sometimes to take a small flask, but I now regard a flask as an offence against tea.) There was no doubt, though, that as I sat on the hill, the shape of the rising sun began to increasingly resemble the shape of a teapot. Another good reason, then, not to doze but to find the homeward path.

I was about to stand up when I heard a voice behind and above me. The voice said, 'Graikk', quite softly, and then, 'Prukk prukk'. I turned slowly to see two ravens circling, or rather swaying back and forth in the light breeze above the ridge. They floated like this for several minutes, talking to each other continually before slanting together overhead and over the edge of the hill. Training the binoculars on them, I watched them levelling off below me, their long wings – as long as a buzzard's – outstretched and the sun glinting on the black plumage as they sailed across the foggy fields. It would have been interesting to have known what they had been discussing.

Only in the last few years have I had the opportunities to regularly listen to the voices of ravens and so
appreciate just how varied they are, so much so that it
seemed obvious, even if I had not read anything on the
subject before, that they had their own quite complex
language. When I first moved into this area I hardly
ever used to see or hear them, but, no doubt benefiting
from their protected status, they gradually increased
over the years until, comparatively recently, I suddenly
began to see them almost every day. Whenever I hear
them cronking and muttering, sometimes in pairs or
groups, they are usually in flight, but occasionally I can
tempt a talkative couple down to the edge of a wood
with some scraps of food. By being patient and keeping
well hidden – a raven's sight is as sharp as any hawk's
– I can then eavesdrop on their guttural but often quite
affectionate-sounding exchanges.

In his book *The Crows* (1978), the ornithologist
Franklin Coombs describes numerous examples of
raven vocabulary, including preening calls, defensive
calls, location calls, aggressive calls, submissive calls,
and different forms of vocal communication between
paired birds and parent and young. To accompany and

possibly to emphasize some of these 'words' the birds also have a wide repertoire of gestures and postures, including ear-tufting, head-flagging, tail-drooping and bowing.

Shepherds and keepers can get unduly tense about ravens because of the bird's occasional habit of killing a weak or sick lamb, yet this behaviour is no more outrageous than a buzzard swooping on a sick or injured rabbit or a peregrine snatching the slowest pigeon in a flock. Personally, I think ravens are the most characterful and interesting of all avians; they are certainly the most intelligent and probably the longest lived, though the ancient Scottish verse quoted by Coombs might stretch the point:

> *Thrice the life of a dog, the life of a horse.*
> *Thrice the life of a horse, the life of a man.*
> *Thrice the life of a man, the life of a stag.*
> *Thrice the life of a stag, the life of a raven.*

If, after life, I were allowed to return to this world in some other form, I would hope to be a bird, just so I could experience the sensation of flight; and if that bird were a raven then I would be able to utter the lovely, sonorous call that the bird only appears to make while soaring so high in a thermal that it is almost out of sight. The call is a distant descending 'Pruuul' that, to my ears, expresses nothing other than joyfulness — joy at having the absolute freedom of the sky.

24

SHAPE-SHIFTER

I walked back the short distance up the slope towards the belt of trees, the rustling of leaves steadily increasing as I climbed. Though the sound seemed surprisingly loud as I pushed between the branches the breeze was no stronger than before, but the previous hour of complete stillness had made the commotion feel as if I had just stepped out of a quiet room onto a station platform. Yet while the sound of the leaves had not changed since first light it had certainly changed since the leaves first appeared, seven weeks ago. I paused a moment amongst the trees because I was suddenly conscious of that difference.

Together with the music of the birds, my favourite spring sound is the breeze-blown susurration of newly unfurled beech leaves. After the thin voices of bare winter trees this fuller breath is as emblematic of spring as the scent of May blossom or the sight of the first swallow. Within a few days, however, the individual leaves have lost their silky transparency, become denser and sharper edged; and now it is midsummer they hiss rather than whisper, a whole tree in the wind making a sound like rolling waves, though the hissing becomes dryer and harsher as autumn approaches.

Beyond the trees, the view south – the terrain of last night's walk – had become completely transformed by the sunlight. The previously shadowy uplands now curved brightly down on either side, the layers of greens and blues separated by the greys and whites of misted valleys. I could just make out the general direction of my homeward path and see, in the far distance, the distinctive shapes of the beech clumps that signalled its end. Setting off southwards through the still-dew-soaked grass (the high breeze had only dried the grass at the very top of the ridge), I retraced my steps round the edge of the hollow and saw below me, on a ledge of natural terracing, four hares – a doe and her three half-grown leverets. I stopped moving, and though I was clearly skylined and only about sixty paces away they remained calmly sitting in the sun. Slowly, I crouched down, slipped the binoculars out of my pocket and focused on them.

Mother was fast asleep. I was looking at her right profile and her large eye was closed, the ears were flat along her back and the legs tightly folded so that she made a compact shape. She looked as if she had just come through a busy night of maternal demands and was now enjoying a well-earned rest. The youngsters were not asleep but quietly nibbling the grass, and though they might have noticed me they had apparently not yet learnt to associate my shape with danger, not that I, personally, wished them harm. It was an image of family bliss, and I was about to lower the glasses and creep away when the mother slowly opened her eye.

For a moment she simply stared, but if she saw my hat and binoculars on the grassy ridge above her, which was all of me that was visible, she didn't care. The leverets continued to graze unconcernedly while she gradually hoisted her long, black-tipped ears. Very slowly and rather stiffly she began to stretch, though it was not like the kind of post-nap stretching I have seen other hares perform. I could imagine the creaking of old bones as she quiveringly extended herself on her long, powerful legs until she was stretched beyond the shape of a hare and into the form of a long, skinny human (like me) standing on all fours. She held that extraordinary position for several moments before relaxing and elegantly refolding herself into a normal sitting position.

Her offspring had moved a little further along the slope while I'd been watching her, but she took no notice of them and began to wash herself. Using her forepaws like a cat, she carefully rubbed her eyes, wiped either side of her nose and scratched the inside of her ears. And while she was thus engaged, I politely withdrew, keeping my head down until I was out of sight.

25

Summer Alchemy

Blackthorn, hawthorn and elder grow well on chalky soil and each has its own month for blossoming. Either standing alone or in thickets they are as vital a link in the ecological chain as a mature oak or a wild-flower meadow, providing nectar for insects, nest sites and berries for songbirds, and sanctuary for smaller mammals and reptiles. Their flowers mark the progress of spring into summer; moreover, elderflower is not just the scent of midsummer, it is the taste.

Walking back through the wood where I saw the fallow deer I caught a faint, familiar smell and sniffed about for a moment until, among a crowd of hazels, I saw a spindly elder tree with a single white disc of blossom. By late June most of the elder bloom has snowed away on the breeze, but there is often a delayed flowering on north-facing slopes, along shady edges of woods or, like this one, in an overgrown clearing. The thin fragrance recalled the more heavily laden shrub I had seen last night; it was not on the path home, but a late gathering of blossom would make the detour worthwhile.

The birdsong still echoed in the trees though it had lost the exultant edge I had heard at first light. In about a fortnight, if I go back again, almost all the songs will have finished for the year, though the woodpigeons will go on cooing till autumn. The deeply shadowed track led out towards the light but when I stepped into the open again I had to mind where I put my feet along the grassy path. After the cool bone-dry weather of the previous few weeks the morning's warm, moist conditions had brought the slugs and snails out to play. There were some big ones, too, amongst a variety of different coloured and patterned specimens, all gliding between the grass blades at a pace I almost envied. If only humanity was similarly incapable of moving any faster than a dawdle there would be endless opportunities for quiet reflection, correspondingly slower clocks and hardly any car crashes. Patience would not be a virtue but a natural condition leading inevitably to universal contentment. And by recognizing its affinity with molluscs, society might stop disparaging them, though song thrushes, toads, slow worms, glow worms and maybe the French would still be allowed to eat them.

The sun was not yet high enough to drive the gastropods from the path, but its beams were causing a mass evacuation nearby. A beech wood stood on the slope ahead, the tall trunks shining silvery down one side, striped with shadow on the other. My detour to the elderflower led through the trees and as I stepped beneath them I could see scores of golden-shelled snails steadily descending, keeping strictly within the shadowline. All night they had been high up, feeding on lichen and fungi, but now the threat of baking sun and murderous birds was forcing them to calmly exit their larder.

I stood watching for a while, interested to see if any individuals oozed faster than others, but none panicked or tried to overtake and the entire snail populace cascaded down the trees at an equal pace, which was about the same rate as cold treacle dripping down the side of a jar.

Beyond the beech trees lay a narrow valley, half in shadow, which I had to cross before I could begin my foraging. As I walked down its grassy slope a crow called out angrily from the wood on the opposite side and several pigeons clattered out of the treetops. Such a commotion is often a sign that a raptor – maybe a peregrine or goshawk – has made an attack, but though I waited a moment after the pigeons had flown nothing else winged into the sky. Perhaps someone had been walking under the trees and I wondered if a figure would appear on the skyline. There was no one, and no more disturbances, so I climbed the opposite slope and eventually found the tree I was looking for.

Last night, when I walked passed the elder, all I could see of it were the pale heads of blossom suspended in moonlight, but daylight revealed it to be a well-shaped little tree, about twelve feet tall, and late to flower as it was partially overshadowed by much larger oaks. Despite limited sunlight it was obviously healthy and productive, making me feel less criminal about picking seven heads from its laden branches. They were all perfect, the individual florets still creamy and full rather than dry and powdery. I carefully pocketed them, intending to separate the florets from the stems when I got home to create an elixir of life.

Centuries ago, alchemists dreamt of mixing such a brew, and had they studied the properties of elderflower they might have woken up to the dream's reality. Rich in all kinds of life-enhancing minerals, it only needs to be stirred into water, honey, lemon and white-wine vinegar to make the most heavenly quaff – or elderflower champagne. Every year I bottle about seven gallons of it, but as fast as I make it family and friends insist on sharing it with me, though this is fine because, being non-alchoholic, each gallon needs to be consumed within a week of bottling. My children have loved it since they were small. Camilla and Alex, the two eldest, are in their mid-twenties now and live far from home, but every midsummer, however busy their lives, they always make time for an elderflower pilgrimage. I shall invite them over next weekend to savour the last floral bubbly of the year.

26

A New Shape
in the Sky

The crow cawed once more and a shadow swung across the grass behind me. A large bird, too large to be the crow, circled above the trees and though I could only glimpse it through the leaves I presumed it was a buzzard until it drifted into the open sky and revealed its identity by its longer wings and distinctive forked tail. It was a red kite and I watched it as it swung gracefully out over the valley, where it was suddenly pounced upon by a trio of rooks who chased it out of sight.

Kites are a new shape in this sky and I only celebrated my first sighting here a few years ago. Nowadays, as with the ravens, I spy them quite regularly, though they are not numerous and there seems to be only one resident pair in the area. The local buzzards, after an initial period of hostility, now seem reconciled to them, but the ravens, like the rest of the corvid family, cannot help their pathological raptor intolerance and the kites live in fear of them.

So much of a bird's character can be revealed by the way it behaves towards another species. A kite is a large, powerful-looking hawk, yet it quails like a mouse if a rook or a jackdaw simply points its beak at it. I had always thought buzzards were equally cowardly when confronted by corvids but last year, as I watched from my garden, I witnessed a wonderful example of buzzard gallantry. A male and female had been soaring together in a thermal but were split up by a squadron of irate rooks who then chased the female into one of the oak trees on the hill opposite. The male circled high over-head for a moment and then vertically dived with such speed and aggressive intent that he scattered his foes to the winds. They did not regroup either but flapped away, keeping low to the ground, looking genuinely shocked. I was quite impressed, but not as much as later that same day when I watched the male having a bath in a sheep trough. For a moment he even lay on his back, with his wings supporting him on the trough's sides, like a man in a bath. Then he preened himself for several minutes before flying up into the oak tree to mate with the female. It would have made a marvellous sequence if only my pal Hugh had been there with his film camera.

I think the crow must have been guarding a nest nearby as it cawed a third time as soon as I stepped out from the shadow of the wood. Cutting back across the shoulder of a hill, I regained the home path and came eventually to the valley where, last night, I thought I heard a swift. As I walked along I kept looking upwards, hoping to see one, and in the blue distance I *did* see one until it flew closer and became a swallow.

Arriving at the last hill I eased the climb by making a long diagonal ascent that brought me up through my favourite group of hawthorns. Last month, dressed in their dense white blossom, they looked like a row of classical ballerinas standing on their points; and there were several different kinds of birds fluttering around them, including a pair of bullfinches – a rare sight nowadays. Every spring the hawthorn flowers lift my heart, every autumn their berries weigh down the birds, yet every winter I grow anxious that the sad craving for order in the farmed landscape will mean their eventual destruction.

In contrast to the breezy uplands, a few miles northward the tall beech clumps in the sheep field stood as silent as I had left them the previous evening. No leaf or branch even quivered and, in the immediate surroundings, there was still no sense of Monday in the air. It seemed an age since dawn, yet judging by the height of the sun it was probably only about breakfast time. I came down the final slope, where the trees overhang my house, walked through the small wilderness of garden and quietly, because people were still asleep upstairs, let myself in.

A FINAL WORD

I first sketched an outline for a book about the night in 1971 and over the next forty years made several attempts at it before finally deciding on its present form – a description of a meandering walk that begins in the evening and ends at sunrise. Friends who read occasional pages from the early drafts were surprisingly encouraging and I'm grateful to them for urging me on towards the final version.

I am particularly indebted to my old art school pal, Ian A. H. Carstairs, for his perceptive reading of the half-completed text. Especially because he understands the natural world better than me (and has spent a lifetime protecting it), his editorial comments and his general enthusiasm for the project were always much appreciated. Thanks are also due to Carol and Roy Sims for their sensitive reading of the opening and closing chapters and their many helpful suggestions.

For their constructive criticism and positive responses I am eternally grateful to Juliette Mitchell, Clare Shepherd, Kevin Parr, Belinda Barrie, Hugh Miles, Clare Hatcher and Sandy Armishawe; and Colin Elford deserves special mention for magicking a treeful of nightjars just when I needed them.

Finally, were it not for a fortuitous meeting between a certain Agent Benham and the publisher Myles Archibald this book would probably have ended up as a lifetime's unfinished essay. Thank you, both.

First published in 2012 by Collins
An imprint of HarperCollins*Publishers*
77–85 Fulham Palace Road
London W6 8JB

www.harpercollins.co.uk

Collins is a registered trademark of
HarperCollins*Publishers* Ltd

15 14 13 12 11 10
10 9 8 7 6 5 4 3 2 1

Text © Chris Yates 2012
Cover illustration © Dan Smith

Chris Yates asserts the moral right to
be identified as the author of this work

A catalogue record for this book is
available from the British Library

ISBN 978-0-00-741554-0

Printed and bound in Great Britain by
Clays Ltd, St Ives plc

MIX
Paper from
responsible sources
FSC
www.fsc.org   **FSC˙ C007454**

FSC™ is a non-profit international organisation established to promote
the responsible management of the world's forests. Products carrying the
FSC label are independently certified to assure customers that they come
from forests that are managed to meet the social, economic and
ecological needs of present and future generations,
and other controlled sources.

Find out more about HarperCollins and the environment at
www.harpercollins.co.uk/green